AF319326

THE BENEVOLENT GASLIGHT

The Benevolent Gaslight

A Technology of Race-Making

Louis M. Maraj & Pritha Prasad

Utah State University Press
LOGAN

© 2026 by University Press of Colorado

Published by Utah State University Press
An imprint of University Press of Colorado
1580 North Logan Street, Suite 660
PMB 39883
Denver, Colorado 80203-1942

All rights reserved

 The University Press of Colorado is a proud member of Association of University Presses.

The University Press of Colorado is a cooperative publishing enterprise supported, in part, by Adams State University, Colorado School of Mines, Colorado State University, Fort Lewis College, Metropolitan State University of Denver, University of Alaska Fairbanks, University of Colorado, University of Denver, University of Northern Colorado, University of Wyoming, Utah State University, and Western Colorado University.

ISBN: 978-1-64642-846-5 (hardcover)
ISBN: 978-1-64642-847-2 (paperback)
ISBN: 978-1-64642-848-9 (ePUB)
ISBN: 978-1-64642-910-3 (PDF)
https://doi.org/10.7330/9781646428489

Library of Congress Cataloging-in-Publication Data
Names: Maraj, Louis Maurice author | Prasad, Pritha author
Title: The benevolent gaslight : a technology of race-making / Louis M. Maraj and Pritha Prasad.
Description: Logan : Utah State University Press, [2026] | Includes bibliographical references and index.
Identifiers: LCCN 2025054652 (print) | LCCN 2025054653 (ebook) | ISBN 9781646428465 hardcover | ISBN 9781646428472 paperback | ISBN 9781646428489 ebook
Subjects: LCSH: Critical discourse analysis | White supremacy (Social structure) | Racism in higher education | Race discrimination | Anti-racism—Study and teaching (Higher) | Social justice—Study and teaching (Higher)
Classification: LCC P302 .M3724 2026 (print) | LCC P302 (ebook)
LC record available at https://lccn.loc.gov/2025054652
LC ebook record available at https://lccn.loc.gov/2025054653

Cover illustration: Desk with hutch belonging to Etta Moten Barnett. Collection of the Smithsonian National Museum of African American History and Culture. Public domain image. A2022.13.1.1ab.

The University Press of Colorado acknowledges the support of the University of Kansas CLAS Book Publishing Assistance Fund toward the publication of this book.

For Mummy, Carolin Gemma Maraj.
Never thought work could ever keep me from grief.

For Mummy, Arti Prasad, and Bauj,
Sudhakar Prasad. Thank you for getting me here.

Contents

Preface

On Race-Making

In his introductory rhetorical theory course, the professor prompts the graduate students present to introduce themselves with their research interests. As Lou rattles off his usual list, a class member, Tom, interrupts: "So like what Pritha does?" In this mundane, reiterative moment of scholarly self-definition, Lou and Pritha merge together marked, racialized, as that-which-is-not. After Lou shares the exchange with Pritha, she emails Tom to express her discomfort with white colleagues essentializing the few students of color in our program—and especially those from distinctly different racial groups like Lou and Pritha. If we don't recognize the field's diverse range of antiracist scholarship, Pritha attests, we further reinforce its "second-class, non-canonical status." This status, emerging from "race" lensed through its dominant white/nonwhite binary, forces those deemed "other" into articulating themselves as pedagogical response. But because Pritha feels guilty for accusing Tom of *maybe* being racist, she softens her message at the end: "I respect you as a colleague, scholar, and equal, and hope that we can all work together as up-and-coming scholars to create a more just

https://doi.org/10.7330/9781646428489.c000a

environment for our students, faculty, and laborers." (Still, as she agonizes over her word choices, she wonders, does Tom feel guilty too? Does he even remember?)

The precarious task of trying to make race *matter* in this dichotomic imaginary (we exist! we are not all the same!) leaves little space for race-*making*, that *making* forever deferred by *mattering*. Energy, in other words, depletes in efforts at attesting to the sheer existence of "the field's diverse range of antiracist scholarship"—and importantly the many unseen, racially marginalized people responsible for it—an exhausting endeavor that itself perpetually precludes that "diverse range" from ever unsettling dialectical racial monoliths. What could race-*making* even look like in schematics of domination that compel us to breathless preoccupation with responding to our own injuries, exclusions, and erasures?

In asserting "respect" for Tom, Pritha concedes to the pace of racial progress, that creation of a "more just environment," to a benevolent vision of her and Tom working "together" (and not because she inherently wants to). When Tom responds, apologizing, he asks whether he and Pritha might meet to help him learn more about "antiracist pedagogy." The delicately crafted, *pedagogical* email offering a learning-for-progress'-sake grace teaches Pritha and her time, space, and labor of their inconceivability. Learning and teaching coalesce into logics that demand racial trauma *be* race-making. Despite the pedagogical energy Pritha has already depleted, Tom's request to meet to help him learn also ensnares Pritha yet again in a pedagogical loop: *So what is the lesson*, he seems to be asking, in response to—quite literally—a lesson? *What can I take away so I can be better?*

The Benevolent Gaslight: A Technology of Race-Making unpacks the historical, epistemological, and cultural logics of racial domination that siphon racial trauma into race-*making*. It asks readers to respond to the question of "lesson" with other questions: What does it mean to read theory beyond extraction and plunder? What does it look like to live *slow* in the *reading*, abandoning quest(ion)s for flecks of citational gold? Who is responsible for race-making differently?

THE BENEVOLENT GASLIGHT

"I Am Not Your Teaching Moment"

In September 2019, *Time* magazine reports the resurfacing of a photo of Canadian prime minister and leader of Canada's Liberal Party, Justin Trudeau, wearing blackface. It shows him dressed in a costume at an "Arabian Nights"-themed party in 2001 at the private day school where he taught (Kambhampaty et al. 2019). The photo—originally published in West Point Grey Academy's yearbook—pictures several others in costume as well but only Trudeau with a painted face. Trudeau, then, when pressed by reporters for other similar incidents in his past during his public apology, reveals that he dressed up in blackface to sing Harry Belafonte's "Day-O" in high school. Later a grainy video from the early 1990s emerges, featuring Trudeau again in blackface flailing his hands in the air and showing his tongue, forcing a second September 2019 apology. The emergence of evidence of public officials' offensive pasts has become almost commonplace in the contemporary public sphere. And while usually associated in North American publics with conservative officials like Virginia Governor Ralph Northam and Alabama Governor Kay Ivey, the particular response from Trudeau

https://doi.org/10.7330/9781646428489.c000b

reveals much about center-left and left-leaning responses to past racist acts and the tendency to eschew blame through a rewriting of history.

Trudeau's initial apology explains, "I shouldn't have done that. I should have known better and I didn't. I'm really sorry." According to *Time* reporters, "When asked if he thought the photograph was racist, he said, 'Yes it was. I didn't consider it racist at the time, but now we know better.'" Propositioned on the possibility of resigning, the Canadian prime minister implored that these incidents be treated on a case-by-case basis, declaring that he has worked "all his life to try and create opportunities for people to fight against racism and intolerance and I can just stand here and say that I made a mistake when I was younger and I wish I hadn't." Trudeau's apology for racist actions, some of which importantly occur in the position of educator, offers avenues for understanding how racial violence—particularly framed through neutral, well-meaning, and even antiracist contexts—can be mobilized for white pedagogical purposes. Racial violences, in essence, become "teaching moments."

While, according to Trudeau, his racist acts did not come from a place of harm in its particular temporality, the shift from "*I didn't consider it racist at the time*" to "now *we* know better" suggests that the individual act, not pursued with racially violent motives in its temporal context, becomes a basis for collective learning—a progression from some (unintentionally?) racist past toward antiracist subjectivity. But who is this "we" that knows better? The Canadian public? White Canadians? Who benefits from the harm of anti-Blackness in this case? While this "we" remains unraced, Trudeau's second apology following the surfacing of video evidence publicizing more of a pattern—rather than one, then two anomalies—begins by him "saying a few words directly to racialized Canadians who face discrimination every single day" (Stephenson and Armstrong 2019). When he evokes a particular audience, racialization seemingly falls only on experiences of nonwhites. Whiteness, in effect, operates invisibly, flexibly, outside of race; as sociologist George Lipsitz (1998, 1) asserts, it need not acknowledge its structural role in sociocultural relations. It is centered, imaginary, invisible.

Like the amorphous "we" of the first apology, Trudeau's tenor in his second, importantly, also highlights the "teaching" of the teaching moment, where the perpetrator of racial violence uses their act not for individual education, but instead to position themself as credible/authoritative on the subject of antiracism. In explaining that "darkening your face, regardless of the context or the circumstances, is *always* [emphasis Trudeau's] unacceptable because of the racist history of blackface," the Canadian prime minister assumes a paternalistic, almost finger-wagging tone. While that tone might register his disappointment with his past self—in his subsequent "I should've understood that then, and I never should have done it"—Trudeau, having identified his audience as racially minoritized Canadians, in preaching to the choir, rhetorically asks for this audience to *accept* the selfsame act he deems *"always"* unacceptable regardless of context/circumstances. So what was offensive in the past happens to manifest itself in the present as a mistake in the now that his listeners can learn from, while his rhetorical framing paradoxically and atemporally washes away his culpability. The audience of Black and Brown Canadians, all too familiar with violence such as Trudeau's, function as the metaphorical fuel for the "lesson."

The Benevolent Gaslight: A Technology of Race-Making understands such workings of racial violence for "productive" pedagogical purposes as a form of *benevolent* gaslighting. While traditionally gaslighting has been a term meant to describe a particular form of interpersonal manipulation in which "the manipulator is trying to get someone else (or a group of people) to question their own reality, memory, or perceptions" (DiGiulio 2018, n.p.), the post-Trump era has underscored the insidiously vast range of forms that gaslighting can take in public and political spheres, with intentions ranging from explicitly violent to progressive or benevolent. In contrast to Trudeau's more "well-intentioned" form of benevolent gaslighting, one might think, for example, of US Counselor to President Trump Kellyanne Conway's infamous usage of the phrase "alternative facts" in 2017 to defend White House Press Secretary Sean Spicer's false statements about the attendance numbers at Trump's inauguration (Blake 2017). The attempted legitimization of false narratives seeks explicitly to distort public memory as political strategy. Trump himself has also gaslit US publics on several occasions. The same year that Conway mentioned "alternative facts," Trump argued that a taped interview with NBC's Lester Holt amid Trump's firing of FBI Director James Comey was doctored to make him look bad (Cillizza 2018), a claim meant to bolster Trump's ongoing attacks against the "fake news media" (Pak and Seyler 2018). Later, during the early days of the COVID-19 pandemic, Trump also repeatedly rejected facts about his administration's own mishandling of the crisis, suggesting that anyone who wants a coronavirus test could get one, even though that statement was at the time blatantly false. He similarly gaslit reporters after he suggested the virus might be treated through the injection of household cleaners into peoples' lungs, claiming he was pranking the press and "asking a question sarcastically to reporters . . . just to see what would happen" (Marcotte 2020, n.p.). Each of these examples—including Trudeau's—deliberately bends and renarrates reality as a way of obscuring the appearance of social or political negligence, regardless of stated political orientation or intention.

In thinking more broadly about gaslighting and its material impacts, we define *benevolent gaslighting* as a technology of race-making—most prominent in the service of white progressivism—that repurposes racist acts as misunderstandings for the sake of all involved. Benevolent gaslighting occurs when those who benefit from whiteness—the processes and structures of racial domination—use violent acts as a teaching tool for universalized progress, while centering the social "good" that might come out of characterizing a (usually past) racist act in the context of its potentials for the "good" that whitenesses/whites have done or might do for marginalized peoples. Apologies like Trudeau's operationalize a *benevolent* form of gaslighting that reshapes racial violence and his role in it as a framework for his continuous work on behalf of minoritized Canadians and for coalescing a past act into a present benefiting from "collective racial progress." It restructures the past through white narratives of teleological development in race relations, through characterizing racist acts as something other than anti-Blackness.

When Trudeau offers that "we" know "better," for example, the "we" suggests a singularity and unity of experience as a way of both obscuring the agent of the act and subsequently establishing collective blame. The obscuration of clusivity—the grammatical distinction between an inclusive and exclusive first-person plural pronoun—allows the agent to appear, through collective voice, as a kind of teacher, rather than an aggressor who perpetuates racial violence and harm. Under *benevolent gaslighting*, injury and harm are imagined as necessary for social and political good. Indeed, if some generalized public learns from racial violence, then it's all good because now "*we* know better." This justifies the embodied harm or injury that occurs along the way, offering a politics of deferral under the hope of a better future. However, does the emergence of a somehow "better" future in which publics have again learned how to be antiracist by someone or something being racist mitigate or justify racialized harm?

The benevolent gaslight and its dual operation of the "teaching moment" are bound up in a narrative of racial progress that proliferates not only in the public and political sphere, but also spaces of knowledge-making, particularly as the university has been increasingly implicated in questions of racial equity and justice.[1] The "teaching moment" in this regard takes up a different meaning, as it is deployed both colloquially *and* pedagogically in the context of the classroom, scholarship, and professionalization. We note the especially prevalent deployment of the teaching moment as an iteration of the *benevolent gaslight* in rhetoric and writing studies, a field that has always been interested in questions of pedagogy and has recently approached—as we discuss more specifically in chapter 1—what many scholars have identified as the "social justice" or "political" turn (Carter et al. 2020, 2). As Shannon Carter, Deborah Mutnick, Stephen Parks, and Jessica Pauszek contend, the political turn in the field calls for a deeper negotiation with "the public and pedagogical role of teachers," and

---

1   See Ahmed (2012) and Kynard (2015).

a deliberate linking of our work as both scholars and teachers to the "insight and strength from historical struggles for social and economic justice in labor, civil rights, Black Power, women's rights, and national liberation struggles" (2). However, as this project shows, the field and the academy more broadly are haunted by their own racial progress narratives that temporally defer materially grounded, antiracist intervention while at the same time suggesting retroactively "learning" from racial violence and injury that has already occurred is a universal and acceptable foundation for developing antiracist politics in teaching and scholarship. If rhetoric and composition has *just* recently entered a "social justice turn," then where do we situate the decades of scholarly and political work by Black, Indigenous, Latinx, and Asian/Asian-American scholars in the field for whom social justice has been not a "turn" but a mode of survival? We pose this question as two racially and culturally marginalized scholars—Pritha, a South Asian woman and second-generation US immigrant, and Lou, a Black immigrant from the Global South—whose critiques, even despite the "social justice turn," continue to be deemed partial, political, and even questionable for whether they are "fair" (as one early reviewer of the article version of this project implied).

The Benevolent Gaslight highlights throughout that the rhetorical process of delinking epistemology from its material impacts—as also the case in the Trudeau example—lies central to its titular concept. Indeed, under the logic Trudeau offers in his apology, the lived and evident racism embodied literally in his past is supposedly unrelated to the antiracist ethos he attests to in the present. Although many critical race, Black feminist, and women of color feminist thinkers and scholars have critiqued this process of epistemic injustice in a wide range of contexts,[2] the conceptualization of the benevolent gaslight primarily focuses on white progressivist pedagogical technologies, institutions, and logics, focusing most specifically upon the pedagogical and epistemological imperatives of intellectual/disciplinary histories of rhetoric

---

2 See Anderson (2017), Collins (2017), Hall (2017), McKinnon (2017), Pitts (2017), Tremain (2017), and Tuana (2017) in *Routledge Handbook of Epistemic Injustice*.

and writing studies, education in the pivotal, historic moment of US Reconstruction, the institutional rhetorics of US colleges and universities, and public and popular culture. The benevolent gaslight does more than just manipulate racialized audiences—it also works to remake, rebrand, and, in many cases, *force* peoples of color (and the violences and racisms we face) into operating *ad infinitum* as educational fodder for white people's personal enlightenment, perpetually deferred "progress," and white imaginaries of social change. The epistemologies that underpin the benevolent gaslight, as discussed at length in chapters 1 and 2, are not limited to the contemporary historical moment, but rather emerge and evolve from a much broader tradition of race-making in the US and Americas from the nineteenth century onward. Our conceptualization of it, however, arose in the post-Ferguson moment when we were two scholars of color newly entering the field of rhetoric and writing studies.[3]

"Benevolent" Origins

As we unpack at length in a *College Conference and Communication* article on which this book project builds, an incident at the 2018 Thomas R. Watson Conference in Louisville, Kentucky, sparked our particular thinking about the race-making gaslighting inherent in public "teaching moments" (Prasad and Maraj 2022). New materialist rhetorical scholar Laurie Gries's utterance of the "n-word" during a conference keynote that year, Gries' subsequent apology, and the consequences of both propelled us to excavate the epistemological grounds making possible the use of that anti-Black act as a platform for Gries's antiracist

---

3　Drawing from Maraj (2020), we define the temporal marker of "post-Ferguson" to refer to "the heightened tensions and public visibility of race relations after the events of the Ferguson Uprising in the summer of 2014." As Maraj posits, these race relations "specifically (re)call attention to tense historical and cultural conversations and protests surrounding Black life and state violence against it" (15). Central to the post-Ferguson moment has also been the public emergence of #BlackLivesMatter directly following the murder of Trayvon Martin in 2013, which was then followed by the police shooting death of Michael Brown in Ferguson, Missouri, in 2014 (Maraj 2020, 15). The "post" in "post-Ferguson" here refers to a shift in dominant racial signification and discourse after the Ferguson Uprising (15).

ethos. At the end of said apology, she resolves to do better and commits to "taking up [her] own challenge" forwarded in her Watson talk: "What if we, especially white people, fully confront our complicity in institutionalized (and other forms of) racism and begin to take direct actions, including collaborating more regularly with people of color and following their leadership, to work against it" (Gries 2018)? The particularly noteworthy shift to a rhetoric of "we" and "our" spotlights a central feature of the benevolent gaslight, as the example of Trudeau also highlights. When she imagines, for instance, what it might look like if "we, especially white people," fully confront "our" complicity in institutionalized racism, one might wonder who she envisions as her apology's audience. Is it those possibly hurt by her actions or those like her who have engaged in acts of racial violence? Her benevolent gaslighting, in this way, establishes an imaginary that makes it acceptable for white people to "make mistakes" just as long as these mistakes can be reframed as a kind of "pedagogy" toward an antiracist subjectivity—the label "antiracist" functioning rhetorically as an *identity* claim rather than a political orientation or action. Further, Gries's imagined collaboration with racially marginalized people make them conditional objects—much like the slur she hurled evokes and extends histories of objectification—for whitened antiracist whims. *The Benevolent Gaslight: A Technology of Race-Making* interrogates these kinds of rhetorical functions of the goodly gaslight and how it makes racialization across different cultural arenas, though it places particular focus on the liberal academy.

The project began as that article in 2019, nearly a year before the 2020 murders of George Floyd, Breonna Taylor, and many others along with widespread nationwide and global protests that followed,[4] the

---

4 On May 25, 2020, in Minneapolis, Minnesota, Black man George Floyd was murdered by police officer Derek Chauvin, an event that led to widespread national protests in solidarity with Floyd and other Black people who had recently been murdered by police, such as Breonna Taylor and Ahmaud Arbery. The murder of Floyd, notably, occurred in the early stages of the COVID-19 pandemic, an illness that is also disproportionately deadly in Black communities (Barone 2020). An autopsy, in fact, later revealed that Floyd had been sick with COVID-19 at the time of his death (Neuman 2020). As Black feminist Brittney Cooper argues in a May 2, 2020, MSNBC interview,

COVID-19 pandemic, and the 2021 anti-Asian Atlanta murders.[5] Since then, a proliferation of statements decrying racism across cultural, political, and educational institutions has been issued. Pritha's institution, the University of Kansas (KU), for instance, released statements "reaffirming" the university's commitment to "inclusivity and respect" after Floyd's murder, contending that "[r]ecent incidents of racial violence underscore the need for us and for all Americans to join together in addressing matters of racism and injustice in a united, meaningful way" (Girod and Bichelmeyer 2020). This statement reads as exhaustingly similar to another released nearly a year later in response to the Atlanta shootings calling for dialogue to make sense of "what is happening" to those "close to us" and "in other communities" (Bankart et al. 2021). Again, as we did after the Gries incident, we wonder: Who is "us"? Who are "all Americans"?

Such institutional rhetorics have come on the heels of hundreds of other similarly empty performances of antiracist intervention, circulated not just by universities but also by major corporations and brands like Amazon, Apple, Google, and countless others throughout 2020 and 2021. Nigerian novelist Ben Okri (2020) even claimed after Floyd's death in *The Guardian*, "This time is different. This time it is epochal." From the years 2013 to 2019, however, between two hundred and three hundred Black people had been killed by police each year ("National Trends" 2020). What about this moment in particular marks it as "different"? Where did this narrative based in a collective conscience and articulated through the universal pronouns "we" and "us"—specifically arising in relation to the murders of Black people, Indigenous people, and people of color—come from?

rhetorics around "reopening" the economy in the wake of COVID-19 are racialized in that they render Black bodies disposable for the sake of economic and capitalist gain (Cooper 2020) As she rightly notes, COVID-19 in this way intersects with anti-Black violence and dehumanization as a form of necropolitics.

5 On March 16, 2021, white man Robert Aaron Long killed eight people at three massage parlors in Atlanta: Delaina Ashley Yaun, Paul Andre Michels, Xiaojie Tan, Daoyou Feng, Hyun Jung Grant, Suncha Kim, and Soon Chung Park, and Yong Ae Yue. Among the eight people Long murdered, six were Asian women. After committing the murders, Long told police that he had a "sexual addiction" and needed to eliminate his "temptation" (Hagen 2021).

The post-Floyd moment teems with instances of racialized violence and death operating as pedagogical fuel for antiracist politics. Consider the widespread circulation of images and videos of Black death as "proof" of anti-Black violence as demonstrated by the mass proliferation of videos of Floyd's murder, of protesters attacked by police with rubber bullets and tear gas, of calls for "listening and support conversations" after the unavoidably gruesome murders of half a dozen Asian women, of white women like Amy Cooper's violent repetition of the same narrative tropes that have historically justified the lynching of Black men and boys (Ore 2019, 4).[6] Once again, racialized injury and death become a basis for collective learning and, as KU's statements attest, joining "together in addressing matters of racism and justice in a united, meaningful way" (Girod and Bichelmeyer 2020). These rhetorics continually recreate linear, cause-and-effect narratives of progress—"this time is different"—in ways that leave little room for upholding, affirming, and mobilizing the antiracist work that has happened before this moment and that will continue to happen after it. They seemingly erase "lessons learned," work done, or histories of racist violence prior to our joining together in this very time. What *matters* seems emergent and consequential rather than situated temporally in the longue durée of transatlantic slavery, of colonialism, or of ongoing ethnic cleansing and genocide.[7] As this book illustrates, identifying the historical and contemporary operations of the benevolent gaslight offers a framework for understanding the multiple competing realities and epistemological tenets in a given moment of racialization turned pedagogical.

---

6 On Monday, May 25, 2020, white woman Amy Cooper, who was walking her dog, called 911 on a bird-watching Black man, Christian Cooper (no relation), who had urged the woman to put her dog on a leash. The situation escalated, and Amy Cooper threatened to call the police and tell them "there's an African American man threatening my life." She eventually did call the police and is now facing charges for falsely reporting an incident (Pereira and Katersky 2020).

7 For a more thorough treatment of how dominant new materialisms' understanding of meaning/matter as "emergent" and "consequential" funds the benevolent gaslight, see Prasad and Maraj (2022).

Defining the Benevolent Gaslight

Historically, the term *gaslighting* can be traced to a 1938 stage play by British playwright Patrick Hamilton that was then popularized in the 1944 film *Gaslight*, which famously stars Ingrid Bergman (Price 2016, 169). This film narrates the story of a woman who unknowingly marries the man who murdered her aunt. In order to access and control the deceased aunt's fortune, the man subsequently works to have his wife confined to psychiatric care by manufacturing small, everyday situations to cause her to question her own memory and perceptions of reality (Ruíz 2014, 201). He gives her gifts only to then steal them and accuse her of losing them; in other moments he misarranges household items as a means for questioning her domestic abilities. Notably, he commits these acts under the guise of moral benevolence as a way of invalidating her own embodied perceptions, memories, and reactions.

Although gaslighting in its original context refers to a mode of psychological or emotional abuse, feminist, critical race, and disability studies scholars discuss the specific operations of gaslighting in the academy. In such spaces, Margaret Price shares, "multiply minoritized faculty, especially those who are queer and/or of color in addition to being disabled" experience gaslighting most frequently (2016, 169). Price narrates the account of a disabled woman and faculty member of color who describes microaggressions she experienced both on the job market and in her job. This faculty member, whom Price refers to as Zoe, recalls her feeling of internalized blame and surveillance as a product of perpetual gaslighting: "It's like, no matter how many degrees you have, you're always worried about being the stereotypical crazy Latina who just has to be a problem" (Price 2016, 164). Elena Flores Ruíz refers to this feeling as a "puncturing self-doubt" that passively polices women of color in the academy, in particular "in the form of normative practices and tacit methodological assumptions" (2014, 201). It forces the cultivation of an "embodied duality" just for means of survival (202).

Our concept of *benevolent gaslighting* follows from Price's (2016) and Ruíz's (2014) work, but the benevolent gaslight works specifically as a *pedagogical* technology mobilized through whiteness to reframe racist acts as meaningful moments of learning, or even teaching, antiracism. In this way, benevolent gaslighting often occurs even with "good intentions"—benevolence operating more as an orientation or affect rather than a deliberate or malicious attempt toward erasure. In benevolent gaslighting, unlike in traditional gaslighting situations in which microaggressions or violences are never acknowledged, the violence *is* acknowledged, though often retroactively and abstractly. This temporally retroactive acknowledgment of violence and its renarration as a "teaching moment" work to justify said racialized violence and its embodied impacts upon racialized groups under the presumed hope of a "better" future in which "this will not happen again" (even as it continues to happen). This linear narrative both renders one's own racism temporally in the past, while at the same time assuming a public audience of white, seemingly inviolable bodies. Trudeau's apology to his multiple instances of blackface makes this evident. The statement of "we know better now" not only assumes a white-bodied audience but also demobilizes negative responses and critiques by racialized audiences, the suggestion being that one cannot—and should not—*still* be mad; the objectification and dehumanization of racialized bodies functions justifiably because violent acts become repurposed for the morally transcendent process of teaching and learning. This framework, however, only allows racialized bodies to appear in social justice work as injured, dead, or stuck in the past rather than as living laborers, cultural producers, scholars, and activists who have always done antiracist work, often behind the scenes and with little recognition. The benevolent gaslighting here functions on two levels: (1) it renarrates racialized violence as pedagogical opportunity; and (2) it invisibilizes the pedagogical, intellectual, and embodied work of racially marginalized peoples by foregrounding white-centered pedagogies of antiracism that may or may not have ever emerged if not in response to a public racist mistake, misstep, or worse.

The abstraction of epistemology from a critical understanding of its material impacts lies at the crux of the *benevolent gaslight*. Intrinsically linked to the body, it works to subtly invalidate one's embodied knowledges and sometimes even one's humanity. In discussing the experience of trans women often subtly gaslit by "allies" through mispronouning and/or misgendering, feminist philosopher Rachel McKinnon contends that gaslighting functions as a form of epistemic injustice. This kind of epistemic violence critically invalidates embodied knowledges and their material realities in ways that can even deny one's existence altogether (McKinnon 2017 169). The benevolent gaslight, then, highlights how race-making rhetorics in the form of speech acts, published pedagogical material, media representations, erasures, historical narratives, and institutional cultures (and other spaces) render the resulting violences as disembodied currency for goodly or "progressive" politics (such as antiracist and "social justice" causes) rather than as harmful modes of denying racially marginalized subjects a situated recognition of their material injury, trauma, or even existence.

Benevolent gaslighting, in highlighting a particular iteration of racialized/racist discourse, relates to previous scholarship on racialized gaslighting outside of rhetorical studies. The notion of "racial gaslighting," a term theorized in 2017 by—and largely credited to—political scientists Angelique M. Davis and Rose Ernst, refers to "the political, social, economic, and cultural process that perpetuates and normalizes a white supremacist reality through pathologizing those who resist" (2019, 47). Racial gaslighting, they attest, relies largely on racial spectacles that "obfuscate the existence of a white supremacist state power structure" (49). Racial spectacles elicit racial responses and influence political decision-making through their deliberate design. They point, for example, to 1990s anti–affirmative action campaigns that weaponized white innocence to "frame the beneficiaries of affirmative action as undeserving" (50), a script forwarded by public media campaigns at the time to establish "a particularly virulent form of racial spectacle" that directly influenced the creation of law (50). Education scholar Ramon Vasquez (2022, 1) similarly theorizes that racial gaslighting in the context of "resilience discourse" is often targeted at BIPOC instructors who are repeatedly told in historically white institutions to "roll with the punches" instead of critiquing or resisting racism. These rhetorics of "resilience," Vasquez argues, "attempt to make BIPOC faculty doubt the persistence and lethalness of systemic racism" (1). Tuesda Roberts and Dorinda J. Carter Andrews (2013), likewise, contend that historical narratives, along with macro-level (such as *Brown vs. Board of Education*) and micro-level (such as state and district-level) educational laws and policies, gaslight African American teachers to believe themselves undesirable and underqualified in the profession. In an analysis of police and news media in Ontario, Canada, Heston Tobias and Ameil Joseph (2020) highlight how local news in Hamilton created a 2015–2016 narrative that facilitated first the profiling of racially marginalized residents and later the evasion of culpability for these actions. Meanwhile, Michelle A. Rodrigues, Ruby Mendenhall, and Kathryn B. H. Clancy (2021) in their *Journal of Women and Minorities in Science and Engineering* study interviewed fifteen women of color science faculty in the US Midwest to unpack how the workplace gaslighting resulting from these women researchers' isolation impact their mental health and job performance. *The Benevolent Gaslight* launches from the intellectual foundation provided by such studies of racialized gaslighting and their material impacts on peoples of color.

Within the field, rhetorician Amy E. Robillard (2023) takes on misogyny in English departments through similar qualitatively driven work as Rodrigues et al., interviewing women in English departments in US colleges and universities. Robillard's framing, however, emphasizes the gender-based discrimination faced by these women through these departments' cultures of obligation and entitlement. Rhetorical studies scholars Clint G. Graves and Leland G. Spencer in a 2022 essay, "Rethinking the Rhetorical Epistemics of Gaslighting," on the other hand, specifically interrogate logocentric, ethotic, and pathetic discursive iterations of "sexist and racist gaslighting" in their analysis of discourses of rape culture and white supremacy. Graves and Spencer aver that gaslighting marks a site of "discursive struggle" (2022, 62) characterized by an uneven dynamic in which "a gaslighter draws on reservoirs of social power to form a caustic appeal structure that 'justifies' belief in their knowledge claims" (61).

Our theory of the benevolent gaslight extends these and other recent scholarly analyses of racial gaslighting. It focuses most specifically on the ways benevolent rhetorics—primarily focused on but not limited to teaching, learning, pedagogy, and progressivism that make racial domination possible—become *weaponized* to *stabilize* discursive struggle and competing truth claims across uneven positions of racial power. While the benevolent gaslight may connect in this way to Davis and Ernst's (2019) and Vasquez's (2022) theorizations, the concept saliently involves the repurposing of racial violence as object lesson for that repurposing's framing as morally "just." The benevolent gaslight—like Davis and Ernst's (2019) model—depends upon a kind of racial spectacle. However, this racial spectacle does not necessarily openly pathologize or demonize peoples of color. Rather, the phenomenon involves the operations of racial domination through public performance of goodly telos as a mechanism for (1) reclaiming such racial dominance in moments of fracture and instability and (2) forwarding whitened visions of "racial justice" that affix whiteness as flexible, agential, and innocent and non-whiteness as infinitely generous, violable, and "resilient"—as Vasquez (2022) points out—yet still (inherently) tragically "flawed," in need of "saving" in the face of the very force that injures it. Benevolent gaslighting, importantly, takes collective "progress" (particularly but not limited to racial "progress") as its justification. This element of the race-making technology can place those it affects at odds with collective or dominant public sentiment for openly resisting it.

So while attitudes toward openly "calling out" interpersonal or even systemic instances of racism—and by extension racialized gaslighting—might arguably appear more relaxed in contemporary North American contexts (than in previous ones), identifying and/or redressing benevolent gaslighting remain/s more difficult. The cultural politics in the proliferation of the term "gaslighting" itself adds to the stickiness of dealing with it. "Gaslighting" as a term has become increasingly widespread as a buzzword in recent years, particularly in popular culture. In 2022, for example, Merriam-Webster named "gaslighting" the "word of the year," stating that "in this age of misinformation—of 'fake news', conspiracy theories, Twitter trolls, and deep fakes—gaslighting has emerged as a word for our time" (Merriam-Webster, n.d.). Headlines like "'Incredible Bulls**t': Anderson Cooper Ripped for 'Gaslighting' over Trump Event" on *HuffPost* (Mazza 2023) or "'They Don't Believe Me': The Pain and Dangers of Medical Gaslighting" on *USA Today* (Yasharoff 2023) make clear the pervasive and almost mundane circulation of the notion. While the popular usage of "gaslighting" may prove generative for giving meaning to the impacts of misinformation and sociopolitical manipulation, many of these mobilizations often individualize it such that it appears to operate more as an interpersonal or even psychologically determined phenomenon, a "communication style" (Oliver 2023), rather than, as *The Benevolent Gaslight* contends, a *historical* and *institutional* force with unique structural impacts for marginalized—but, specifically, racialized—groups.

Education scholars J. Luke Wood and Frank Harris II's attempted popularization of "racelighting," in fact, emphasizes this interpersonal angle into racialized gaslighting. In contextualizing these endeavors in the post-Floyd moment when "millions of people have expressed a desire to build a more harmonious [US] nation," their concept provides space for "racial reckoning" by "coming to terms with" the country's "historical ills" (2021, 4). They build particularly on previous scholarly theorizations of racialized gaslighting, especially Rodrigues et al.'s (2021) study, to highlight what they apprehend as interpersonal and quotidian about this kind of gaslighting (Wood and Harris 2021, 10). In doing so, they offer racelighting as "the process whereby [p]eople of [c]olor question their own thoughts and actions due to systematically delivered racialized messages that make them second guess their own lived experiences [and realities] with racism." As a public-facing project, Woods and Harris deploy a website (racelighting.net), lesson plans, and YouTube and TikTok videos, while uptake of the concept in academia has resulted in publications like the journal *Equality, Diversity, and Inclusion*'s special issue titled "You Can't Racelight Critical Race Theory!" (Smith and Parker 2024). Benevolent gaslighting, though, describes more than just isolated moments or examples of gaslighting and instead constitutes a deeply entrenched epistemology for US racial politics, temporalities of "progress," and public pedagogies of racializing dominance. A discursive and epistemological framework writ large, it sets the terms of racial engagement and recognition across popular culture, academia, protest, and politics. Crucially, its "common cause" telos in race relations reinforces and technologizes linear historical narratives that make possible even *more* benevolent gaslighting to come.

In articulating the benevolent gaslight as a *technology* rather than merely a rhetorical device, this project captures its distinct movement and plasticity as a narrative, historical, and cultural apparatus. Like Black and new media studies scholar Beth Coleman, we understand race as itself a "levered mechanism" (Coleman 2009, 180) that takes up variable meaning across time, space, and context. Conceptualizing race as a technology, Coleman offers, enables a study of race beyond its social-constructedness as an identity or trait. Race, as a tool, shapes patterns of meaning, materiality, and power (185). Our explication of the benevolent gaslight as a *technology* of race-*making*, then, captures the phenomenon's mobility and capaciousness across the case studies—both contemporary and historical—that structure this book.

For example, consider how the rhetoric of the "teaching moment" evident in apologies like those of Trudeau and Gries works as a technology for making only certain visions/versions of racialized bodies visible. "We know better now" as a racial progress narrative (often deployed) in the context of anti-Black violence holds deep roots in a Middle Passage epistemology and a chronological narrative of Blackness that understands racial progress as a series of linear victories over *anti*-Blackness (Wright 2015, 47). Each event in this progress narrative—in locating the origin of Blackness in the West first and foremost in US and European slave ships—always refers, Michelle

Wright affirms, to triumphs over white obstacles, tying Black agency to white racist actions. Black actions, then, function always as *reactions*, rendering Black agency and existence highly contingent rather than a "celebrated given." In this way, if racism operates epistemologically as pedagogical technology for whiteness to overcome its own violence, these forces making racial domination deem the humanity of those racially minoritized not only perpetually violable, but also visible only in moments of white violence. Temporally, such a framework of injury-response leaves little room to understand the daily and historical resistance work of those who have faced centuries of enslavement and colonialism to define their humanity outside of—and in response to—the liberal humanism that continues to render racialized, nonwhite bodies as inhuman or contingent.[8]

This schema also plays out in dominant popular, political, and economic discourses surrounding racialized violences. Even as Movement for Black Lives (MBL) and Black Lives Matter (BLM) continue to organize in moments beyond the widely publicized murders of Black people like Michael Brown, George Floyd, and Breonna Taylor, corporations and politicians typically do not publicly articulate (performative) solidarity (Cohen 2014) with Black movements *until* a high-profile murder occurs. In these cases, white supremacist agencies exclusively necessitate the affirmation of Black Lives Matter and that Black people and their lived experiences do, in fact, matter. What appears, then, as racial "progress" in the form of dominant institutions "finally" recognizing the prevalence of anti-Blackness operates instead in the service of whiteness restabilizing and positioning itself to "dictate the pace of racial progress" (Cooper 2016, n.p.) and "master—and become master of—time" (Mills 2007, 31). The benevolent gaslight obscures these temporal and structural dimensions of race-making through frameworks that dually individuate racisms (like the hyper-focus on Floyd's death, for example) as isolated "teaching moments" and easily corral them into racial progress narratives highlighting the goodliness of single actors, collectives, and even cultural trends.

---

8 See Weheliye (2014).

Method and Scope

The Benevolent Gaslight: A Technology of Race-Making unfolds through a case-study-like attendance to varied functions and forces of its titular concept across different spatialities and temporalities. Its three more "traditional" chapters undertake analysis of the gaslight in specific historical, epistemological, and cultural arenas with an eye toward revealing the workings of racialized manipulation in a diverse set of artifacts—ranging from nineteenth-century pedagogical manuals to university presidents' statements in the age of #BlackLivesMatter. Its fourth, experimental chapter takes a markedly creative, narrative-based approach to offer means to grasp the technology as method/mode of interpretation; it puts the onus on readers to identify how the benevolent gaslight exists, spreads, and mutates indiscreetly in popular and political thought and media representations. Paying attention to the particular but interconnected iterations of the gaslight across the monograph's breadth involves engagement with not just rhetorical studies but scholarship from a host for interrelated fields. Readers will find links with history, gender and sexuality studies, Black studies, and critical race and ethnic studies, with sustained theoretical discussion through Black feminist thought, women of color feminisms, critical theory, and decolonial frameworks. And though whiteness appears throughout as an important point of critical departure, this study does not deploy whiteness studies as one of its interpretive frames. It prioritizes, instead, impacts on nonwhite subjects in whiteness's making and marking modes of racial domination.

Because gaslighting as a phenomenon entails (to some degree) the manipulation of actions, histories, and narratives into particular temporal arrangements, the arguments herein take a keen and careful approach to how they treat histories as they relate to the experiences of racially marginalized subjects. Rather than situating the project in relation/reaction to (US) conservative outcry around "presentism"[9]—

---

9 "Presentism" refers to the presentation and interpretation of historical events via contemporary phenomena and lenses. Some claim it distorts "true" accounts of history by

one might glance at the response to Nikole Hannah-Jones's *1619 Project* or the far-right war on "critical race theory" since 2020 for a taste of this sentiment[10]—*The Benevolent Gaslight* shares, instead, a highly contextualized, materially grounded, critical stance on notions of temporality and dominant "linear" constructs of history. Aligned with intellectual work emanating from, and in epistemological concert with, Saidiya Hartman's conception of "the afterlives of slavery" (2007, 6)—such as Christina Sharpe's (2016) *In the Wake: On Blackness and Being*—*The Benevolent Gaslight* understands the still-extant iterations of the *longue durée* of transatlantic slavery and European colonialism as beyond mere historical shadows/vestiges in its twenty-first-century moment. The study considers the narrative and temporal control of such iterations for morally "just" purposes (distinctly articulated for the "benefit" of the controlled) as its purview.

"Racial Forgetting/White Time: The Benevolent Gaslight in Disciplinary Knowledge-Making," the first chapter, surveys a range of material—from scholarship to epistemological trends to pedagogical developments—to show how rhetoric, composition, and English studies rely on racist violence across the twentieth century for its socioracial "progression." Rhetoric and writing studies, in particular, take inspiration from racial injury to prompt and chart the major shifts in that field's collective thinking, specifically the "social justice" or "political" turns of the early twenty-first century. The historicizing of the field in this way produces temporal schema that disappear past and ongoing antiracist and decolonial scholarly, pedagogical, community-building, and activist labor of its Black, Indigenous, Latinx, and Asian/Asian-American scholars/teachers.

---

introducing present-day "cultural bias." We understand this concept as resting on the notion that whiteness entitles itself alone to "objectivity" without recognizing its own lenses as inherently culturally biased. For more on the historical and scientific construction of whiteness as transparent/objective, see Ferreira da Silva (2007).

10 These claims may seem ironic given that some conservatives, such as those involved in the Tea Party movement that began in 2009, adhere to tenets of "originalism"—the literal reading of the US Constitution without regard for the nuances of context, times, and places of its application.

"I AM NOT YOUR TEACHING MOMENT"

Prompted by the early 2020s trend in rhetorical studies—as well as popular investments in other humanities and social science disciplines—in the language of "abolition" as a mode of social-justice-oriented thinking, *The Benevolent Gaslight*'s second chapter delves into discursive politics with/in the historical moment of the US abolition of slavery. "Violent (Re)construction(s): Gaslighting 'Abolition' in US Educational History" underscores the long arc of the benevolent gaslight as a function of Western racialization. It analyzes early Reconstruction pedagogical texts, first published between 1864 and 1866 and written by white, abolition-minded figures specifically for an audience of newly freed Black learners. In so doing, the chapter shows how the works of Clinton Bowen Fisk, Rev. Jared Bell Waterbury, and Lydia Maria Child offer this audience a pedagogy that emphasizes a burdening "individual responsibility" along rhetorical structures that recharacterize slavery's institutions and violences as a teaching moment in the service of collective US nation-building. Though often celebrated for their historical contributions to the "progress" of Black peoples—especially Child, an inductee of both the National Women's Hall of Fame and the National Abolition Hall of Fame—"Violent (Re)construction(s)" calls into question the goodly activist "abolitionist" and the resultant idea of "abolitionist pedagogy." It throws into disarray understandings of early US education of the racially marginalized and the white "heroes" who facilitated their goodliness still set in historical stone.

Chapter 3, "Benevolent Diversity: Student Protest and Institutional Gaslighting," returns to the site of the twenty-first-century university and its culture's fertile grounds for commodifying teaching, learning and associated activities. Within these cultures, the chapter illustrates how those educational spaces wield "legitimate" teaching and learning as means to mark student activism "illegitimate." Though the post-2020 rush to "racial reckoning" assisted a marked increase in these binarizing discourses, "Benevolent Diversity" spotlights how the concurrent romanticization and curated misrepresentation of

Civil Rights and post–Civil Rights student activisms—movements largely responsible for US universities' "diversity" and "equity"-based investments—lay the foundation for said discourses. Unpacking the 2019 #NotAgainSU student protests at Syracuse University and its administration's response exemplifies how historically white universities resultingly produce spotless, linear progress narratives as their dominant histories. These narratives work to benevolently gaslight racially marginalized students, staff, and faculty, policing their reactions to campus violence while criminalizing those who resist.

"No, but This Actually Happened," the concluding chapter, explodes contemporary instantiations and contexts for the benevolent gaslight beyond the frame of educational spaces proper, Global North contexts and subjects, and its emanation from bodies phenotypically raced white. Exposing how the technology permeates public and popular discourse, the chapter interweaves examples and consumable cultural commonplaces to reveal the insidious extensions of this kind of racializing manipulation. Through a creative, narrative-based version of inter(con)textual reading (Appadurai 1996, Hesford 2011, Maraj 2020), "No, but This Actually Happened" invites its audience into thinking with/in the benevolent gaslight as hermeneutic. The conclusion's purview ranges pop culture discourse, governmental responses to protest, media coverage of climate change, and more. Criss-crossing nonfictional and fictional representations and lived experiences, the chapter unmoors linear, temporally hegemonic, and genre-based constructions of "reality" to inherently question their formations. Ending on this note, *The Benevolent Gaslight: A Technology of Race-Making* proposes that its audiences seize how narrative frames (and their possible arrangements) simultaneously hold potentials to reproduce, concretize, reinvent, yet confront and challenge its nominal mode of racialization. Such departure eschews popular prescriptive, step-by-step-guide interventions to destabilizing racial hierarchies that often result in commodifying antiracism, making it fuel for extractive, colonial schema. Ultimately, it offers no "lesson(s)" from the violences engaged to challenge moral-based reads of race-making trauma. "So What Is the lesson?"—a reflective/reflexive echo, prompted by a peer review of this project—bookends the final chapter by (critically and temporally) leaning into the rejection of such interpretive imperatives.

While some may criticize a study like this one as "diagnostic," suggesting that beside critique it offer a path forward as well, we refuse this suggestion as a point of fidelity. Dominant cultures make the benevolent gaslight possible precisely because they demand "progress," linear senses of cause-and-effect, and that racial violences produce some*thing* they might learn from and/or teach with. Again, we refuse. As proven by the artifacts, rhetorical situations, lived experiences, and so forth that we analyze, racial violence breeds anew from this mode of thinking. This introduction and this monograph departs instead, as *The Benevolent Gaslight* in toto ends, by posing the crucial and reiterative question: With whom does and should responsibility lie for race-making outside of (narrative) frames of racial violence?

References

Ahmed, Sara. 2012. *On Being Included: Racism and Diversity in Institutional Life.* Durham, NC: Duke University Press.

Anderson, Luvell. 2017. "Epistemic Injustice and the Philosophy of Race." In *Routledge Handbook of Epistemic Injustice*, edited by Ian James Kidd, José Medina, and Gaile Pohlhaus Jr., 139–148. New York: Routledge.

Appadurai, Arjun. 1996. *Modernity at Large: Cultural Dimensions of Globalization.* Minneapolis: University of Minnesota Press.

Bankart, Charles A. S., D. A. Graham, and Derek Kwan. 2021. "RE: Statement of Support for Our Asian and Asian-American Community." Received by Pritha Prasad. March 18, 2021.

Barone, Emily. 2020. "COVID-19 Isn't the First Pandemic to Affect Minority Populations Differently. Here's What We Can Learn From the 1918 Flu." *Time*, August 7. https://time.com/5877004/covid-black-americans-1918-flu/.

Blake, Aaron. 2017. "Kellyanne Conway Says Donald Trump's Team Has 'Alternative Facts': Which Pretty Much Says It All." *Washington Post*, January 22. https://www.washingtonpost.com/news/the-fix/wp/2017/01/22/kellyanne -conway-says-donald-trumps-team-has-alternate-facts-which-pretty-much -says-it-all/.

Carter, Shannon, Deborah Mutnick, Steve Parks, and Jessica Pauszek. 2020.

"Introduction: What Does Democracy Look Like?" In *Writing Democracy: The Political Turn In and Beyond the Trump Era*, edited by Shannon Carter, Deborah Mutnick, Steve Parks, and Jessica Pauszek, 1–23. New York: Routledge.

Cillizza, Chris. 2018. "Donald Trump Just Keeps Claiming Things He Said on Tape Aren't Real." CNN, August 30. https://www.cnn.com/2018/08/30/politics/trump-lester-holt-nbc/index.html.

Cohen, Cathy. 2014. "#DoBlackLivesMatter? From Michael Brown to CeCe McDonald on Black Death and LGBTQ Politics." Lecture, December 2. New York. http://www.racismreview.com/blog/wp-content/uploads/2014/12/Cohen_CLAGS_Transcript_121214.pdf.

Coleman, Beth, 2009. "Race As Technology." *Camera Obscura* 70 (2.1): 177–207. https://doi.org/10.1215/02705346-2008-018.

Collins, Patricia Hill. 2017. "Intersectionality and Epistemic Injustice." In *Routledge Handbook of Epistemic Injustice*, edited by Ian James Kidd, José Medina, and Gaile Pohlhaus Jr., 115–124. New York: Routledge.

Cooper, Brittney. 2016. "The Racial Politics of Time." Filmed October 2016 in San Francisco, CA. TED Video, 12:20. https://www.ted.com/talks/brittney_cooper_the_racial_politics_of_time/transcript.

Cooper, Brittney. 2020. "Coronavirus Outcomes Worse for People of Color as States Reopen." *MSNBC*, May 2. https://www.msnbc.com/am-joy/watch/coronavirus-outcomes-worse-for-people-of-color-as-states-reopen-82945093590.

Davis, Angelique M., and Rose Ernst. 2019. "Racial Gaslighting." *Politics, Groups, and Identities* 7 (4): 761–774. https://doi.org/10.1080/21565503.2017.1403934.

DiGiulio, Sarah. 2018. "What Is Gaslighting?" NBCNews.com, July 13. www.nbcnews.com/better/health/what-gaslighting-how-do-you-knowif-it-s-happening-ncna890866.

Ferreira da Silva, Denise. 2007. *Toward a Global Idea of Race*. Minneapolis: University of Minnesota Press.

Girod, Douglas, and Barbara A. Bichelmeyer. 2020. "RE: A Message to the KU Community." Received by Pritha Prasad, June 2, 2020.

Graves, Clint G., and Leland G. Spencer. 2022. "Rethinking the Rhetorical Epistemics of Gaslighting." *Communication Theory* 32 (1): 48–67. https://doi.org/10.1093/ct/qtab013.

Gries, Laurie. 2018. "Dear Watson Conference Organizers, Participants, and Audience Members of My Keynote Address." Received by Watson Conference attendees, November 28, 2018.

Hagen, Lisa. 2021. " 'Sex Addiction' Cited as Spurring Spa Shooting, But Most Killed Were of Asian Descent." NPR, March 17. https://www.npr.org/2021/03/17/978288270/shooter-claimed-sex-addiction-as-his-reason-but-most-victims-were-of-asian-desce.

Hall, Kim Q. 2017. "Queer Epistemology and Epistemic Injustice." In *Routledge Handbook of Epistemic Injustice*, edited by Ian James Kidd, José Medina, and Gaile Pohlhaus Jr., 158–166. New York: Routledge.

Hartman, Saidiya. 2007. *Lose Your Mother: A Journey Along the Atlantic Slave Route*. New York: Farrar, Straus and Giroux.

Hesford, Wendy S. 2011. *Spectacular Rhetorics: Human Rights Visions, Recognitions, Feminisms*. Durham, NC: Duke University Press.

Kambhampaty, Anna Purna, Madeleine Carlisle, and Melissa Chan. 2019. "Photo Shows Justin Trudeau in Brownface at 'Arabian Nights' Party." *Time*, September 18. time.com/5680759/justin-trudeau-brownface-photo/.

Kynard, Carmen. 2015. "Teaching While Black: Witnessing and Countering Disciplinary Whiteness, Racial Violence, and University Race-Management." Literacy in Composition Studies 3 (1): 1–20. https://doi.org/10.21623/1.3.1.16.

Kynard, Carmen. 2014. *Vernacular Insurrections: Race, Black Protest, and the New Century in Composition-Literacies Studies*. Albany: State University of New York Press.

Lipsitz, George. 1998. *The Possessive Investment in Whiteness: How White People Profit from Identity Politics*. Philadelphia: Temple University Press.

Maraj, Louis M. 2020. *Black or Right: Anti/Racist Campus Rhetorics*. Logan: Utah State University Press.

Marcotte, Amanda. 2020. "Gaslighting on Lysol-gate: Now Trump Is Denying He Said What We Heard Him Say." Salon, April 27. https://www.salon.com/2020/04/27/gaslighting-on-lysol-gate-now-trump-is-denying-he-said-what-we-heard-him-say/.

Mazza, Ed. 2023. " 'Incredible Bulls**t': Anderson Cooper Ripped for 'Gaslighting' over Trump Event." Huffington Post, May 12. https://www.huffpost.com/entry/anderson-cooper-trump-town-hall_n_645da32ce4b005be8ff2a438.

McKinnon, Rachel. 2017. "Allies Behaving Badly: Gaslighting as Epistemic Injustice." In *Routledge Handbook of Epistemic Injustice*, edited by Ian James Kidd, José Medina, and Gaile Pohlhaus Jr., 167–174. New York: Routledge.

Merriam-Webster. n.d. "Word of the Year 2022." https://www.merriam-webster.com/wordplay/word-of-the-year-2022.

Mills, Charles W. 2007. "White Ignorance." In *Race and Epistemologies of Ignorance*, edited by Shannon Sullivan and Nancy Tuana, 11–38. Albany: State University of New York Press.

"National Trends." 2020. Mapping Police Violence. https://mappingpolice violence.us/nationaltrends.

Neuman, Doug. 2020. "Medical Examiner's Autopsy Reveals George Floyd Had Positive Test for Coronavirus." NPR, June 4. https://www.npr.org/sections/live-updates-protests-for-racial-justice/2020/06/04/869278494/medical-examiners-autopsy-reveals-george-floyd-had-positive-test-for-coronavirus.

Okri, Ben. 2020. "'I Can't Breathe': Why George Floyd's Words Reverberate Around the World." *The Guardian*, June 8. https://www.theguardian.com/commentisfree/2020/jun/08/i-cant-breathe-george-floyds-words-reverberate-oppression.

Oliver, David. 2023. "Feeling Like You've Been Subtly Tricked? It Might Be 'Ambient Gaslighting.'" *USA Today*, March 28. https://www.usatoday.com/story/life/health-wellness/2023/03/28/ambient-gaslighting-manipulation-definition-explained/11514894002/.

Ore, Ersula J. 2019. *Lynching: Violence, Rhetoric, and American Identity*. Jackson: University of Mississippi Press.

Pak, Nataly, and Matt Seyler. 2018. "Trump Calls 'Fake News' Media 'The Real Enemy of the People' over Putin Summit." ABC News, July 19. https://abcnews.go.com/Politics/trump-calls-fake-news-media-real-enemy-people/story?id=56687436.

Pereira, Ivan, and Aaron Katersky. 2020. "Amy Cooper Charged in Central Park False Report Against Black Bird Watcher." ABC News, July 6. https://abcnews.go.com/US/amy-cooper-charged-central-park-false-report-christian/story?id=71635157.

Pitts, Andrea J. 2017. "Decolonial Praxis and Epistemic Injustice." In *Routledge Handbook of Epistemic Injustice*, edited by Ian James Kidd, José Medina, and Gaile Pohlhaus Jr., 149–157. New York: Routledge.

Prasad, Pritha, and Louis M. Maraj. 2022. "I Am Not Your Teaching Moment: The Benevolent Gaslight and Epistemic Violence." *College Composition and Communication* 74 (2): 322–351.

Price, Margaret. 2016. "Un/Shared Space: The Dilemma of Inclusive Architecture." In *Disability, Space, Architecture: A Reader*, edited by Jos Boys, 155–172. New York: Routledge.

Roberts, Tuesda, and Dorinda J. Carter Andrews. 2013. "A Critical Race Analysis of the Gaslighting Against African American Teachers: Considerations for Recruitment and Retention." In *Contesting the Myth of a 'Post Racial' Era: The Continued Significance of Race in U.S. Education*, edited by Dorinda J. Carter Andrews and Franklin Tuitt, 69–96. Lausanne, Switzerland: Peter Lang Publishers.

Robillard, Amy E. 2023. *Misogyny in English Departments: Obligation, Entitlement, Gaslighting*. Lausanne, Switzerland: Peter Lang Publishers.

Rodrigues, Michelle A., Ruby Mendenhall, and Kathryn B. H. Clancy. 2021. "'There's Realizing, and Then There's Realizing': How Social Support Can Counter Gaslighting of Women of Color Scientists." *Journal of Women and Minorities in Science and Engineering* 27 (2): 1–23.

Ruíz, Elena Flores. 2014. "Musing: Spectral Phenomenologies: Dwelling Poetically in Professional Philosophy." *Hypatia* 29 (1): 196–204.

Sharpe, Christina. 2016. *In the Wake: On Blackness and Being*. Durham, NC: Duke University Press.

Smith, William A., and Laurence Parker. 2024. "Guest Editorial: You Can't Racelight CRT!" *Equality, Diversity, and Inclusion* 43 (3): 389–399.

Stephenson, Mercedes, and James Armstrong. 2019. "EXCLUSIVE: Video Shows Trudeau in Blackface in 3rd Instance of Racist Makeup." Global News, September 19. globalnews.ca/news/5922861/justin-trudeau-brownface-video /?utm_medium=Facebook&utm_source=GlobalNews.

Tobias, Heston, and Ameil Joseph. 2020. "Sustaining Systemic Racism Through Psychological Gaslighting: Denials of Racial Profiling and Justifications of Carding by Police Utilizing Local News Media." *Race and Justice* 10 (4): 424–455.

Tremain, Shelly. 2017. "Knowing Disability, Differently." In *Routledge Handbook of Epistemic Injustice*, edited by Ian James Kidd, José Medina, and Gaile Pohlhaus Jr., 175–183. New York: Routledge.

Tuana, Nancy. 2017. "Feminist Epistemology." In *Routledge Handbook of Epistemic Injustice*, edited by Ian James Kidd, José Medina, and Gaile Pohlhaus Jr., 125–138. New York: Routledge.

Vasquez, Ramon. 2022. "You Just Need More Resilience: Racial Gaslighting as 'Othering.'" *Journal of Critical Thought and Praxis* 11 (3): 1–14.

Weheliye, Alexander G. 2014. *Habeas Viscus: Racializing Assemblages, Biopolitics, and Black Feminist Theories of the Human*. Durham, NC: Duke University Press.

Wright, Michelle M. 2015. *Physics of Blackness: Beyond the Middle Passage Epistemology*. Minneapolis: University of Minnesota Press.

Wood, Luke J., and Frank Harris II. 2021. *Racelighting in the Normal Realities of Black, Indigenous, and People of Color: A Scholarly Brief*. San Diego: Community College Assessment Lab.

Yasharoff, Hannah. 2023. "'They Don't Believe Me': The Pain and Dangers of Medical Gaslighting." *USA Today*, May 19. https://www.usatoday.com/story /life/health-wellness/2023/05/19/medical-gaslighting-patients-doctors -need-to-know/70232820007/.

1 · Racial Forgetting/White Time

The Benevolent Gaslight in Disciplinary Knowledge-Making

In 2020, just months after George Floyd's murder, white associate professor of history at George Washington University Jessica Krug penned a public letter and apology for pretending to be Black for the majority of her adult life. "I have eschewed my lived experience as a white Jewish child in suburban Kansas City under various assumed identities within a Blackness I had no right to claim," she admits (Krug 2020). Throughout the years, she identified as a range of Black identities: North African Black, US-rooted Black, Caribbean-rooted Bronx Black. In a "masterful" performance of shame and guilt, she confesses:

> People have fought together with me and have fought for me, and my continued appropriation of a Black Caribbean identity is not only, in the starkest terms, wrong—unethical, immoral, anti-Black, colonial—but it means that every step I've taken has gaslighted those whom I love. (Krug 2020, n.p.)

A separate essay could very well be written about the racial gaslighting of a white person strategically altering their appearance and crafting

 https://doi.org/10.7330/9781646428489.c001

their word choices to pretend to be Black, to earn the trust of Black people and other people of color, and to claim structural oppression. More relevant here, however, is the way that Krug and others like her importantly embody a very particular extreme of white dominance—one that at once centers whiteness while also attempting quite literally to obliterate it. In her apology letter, for example, even as she acknowledges that "intention never matters more than impact," Krug locates the origins of her insidious racial performance in "unaddressed mental health demons" and "severe trauma that marked my early childhood and teen years." Aside from the ableist assertion that mental disability and trauma lead to racist acts, even in the face of being nationally exposed as a racist, Krug stunningly refuses to state the obvious: Her actions plainly articulate white supremacy.

After Krug had been publicly outed, the Black people who knew Krug reflected on their longstanding feelings of embodied unease in their interactions with her. Black writer and activist Hari Ziyad, for example, wrote in *Vanity Fair* in 2020 about how Krug's single-dimensioned performance of Blackness routinely fetishized pain and trauma. Ziyad remembers how Krug embraced an ideology that positioned Black liberation "as a thing demanding misery and loneliness," which often meant that she would attack Black people constantly, accusing Ziyad's Black friends of being "gentrifiers and middle-class interlopers" and castigating them for "failing to be revolutionaries" (Ziyad 2020, n.p.).

Ziyad notes that this flat, fetishized performance of Blackness/Black pain specifically led Black people to both question Krug's Blackness and feel unsafe around her. Just before Krug was outed for being white, she called Ziyad in a panic: "She rambled about how she's been lying about something for a very long time and it's going to come out soon and she's sorry, but she swears she's 'not like Shaun King or Rachel Dolezal' because she actually loves Black people."[1] However, despite

---

1 In June 2015, Rachel Dolezal, a white woman from Montana, was exposed for pretending to be Black. Dolezal worked as an instructor of African studies at Eastern Washington University and had also served as president of the National Association for the Advancement of Colored People (NAACP) in Spokane, Washington, before being removed from that position after being outed as white (McGreal 2015). Shortly after

her insistence, Ziyad claims that "Jess was not different from any of those imposters." All these people "see Blackness as unworthy of love, as unworthy of complexity, unworthy of joy and leisure and having boundaries that are exclusive of anyone who arms them, least of all white people like them" (Ziyad 2020, n.p.). Indeed, white racial frauds who have pretended to be Black share this common theme. C. V. Vitolo, for example, a white PhD student of journalism and mass communication at the University of Wisconsin in Madison who infiltrated activist circles while pretending to be Black at the same time as Krug, also mobilized a fetishistic performance of Blackness that equated it directly with harm and violence. Vitolo, like Krug, gaslit colleagues and activists by painting themselves as a victim of racism whenever anyone attempted to question their racial identity (Anonymous 2020).

Although dominant news narratives surrounding Krug and Vitolo describe their proximity to the academy as incidental to their violent racial performances, that proximity, serves as *central* to those performances. The whitestream and academic fetishization of racial pain has in fact gained unique traction in the post-Ferguson moment.[2] In said moment, anti-Black and racial violences have not only dominated, but also actively initiated, popular and—importantly—academic "reckonings" with racism. This business of "coming to terms with racism" may not have otherwise occurred or received widespread interest without the widely reported and/or visually documented murders of Black men and boys like Michael Brown, Eric Garner, Freddie Gray, Tamir Rice, and George Floyd. Beyond widespread circulation of videos of Black death and violence as "proof" of the reality of anti-Blackness, the sudden increase of academic and scholarly inquiries into race and racism

---

Dolezal was exposed, rumors began to circulate about Black Lives Matter activist Shaun King after his birth certificate showed that both of his birth parents were white and he was therefore not biracial, as he had previously claimed. King claims the father listed on his birth certificate is not his actual father and that his father is a Black man whom he does not know (Lowery and Miller 2015).

2   See Grande (2003) for an expanded discussion of "whitestream" theory, which Grande discusses in the context of mainstream feminist theory. "Whitestream" refers to discourse that is principally structured on the basis of "white, middle-class experience" that serves white ethno-political interests and capital investments (329).

     RACIAL FORGETTING/WHITE TIME

in the form of professional organization position statements, race/racism-themed special issues, social justice–themed conferences, and "antiracist" university diversity and inclusion programming evidences this fetishistic pattern. Anti-Blackness and racism have become both pedagogical fodder for "antiracism," as theorized in the benevolent gaslight, as well as an epistemological basis for *defining* normative (and reductive) conceptions of nonwhite racial identities, as both Krug and Vitolo demonstrate. In other words, in this rhetorical schema, normative recognition or discussion of nonwhite racial identities and/or racism occur primarily with the violent targeting and/or killing of people of color—a phenomenon that fetishizes and commodifies racial pain as productive inspiration for racial justice work.

While these contexts and narratives have shaped theoretical and epistemological trends in the humanities proper, it appears specifically evident in dominant circles of rhetoric and writing studies. In the wake of—and in response to—Ferguson and, more recently, Floyd/Minneapolis, many scholars in the field propose this disciplinary moment as constituting a "social justice" or "political turn." Take, for example, Mya Poe, Asao B. Inoue, and Norbert Elliot's 2018 volume, *Writing Assessment, Social Justice, and the Advancement of Opportunity*; Rebecca Walton, Kristen Moore, and Natasha Jones's 2019 monograph, *Technical Communication After the Social Justice Turn*; and Shannon Carter, Deborah Mutnick, Stephen Parks, and Jessica Pauszek's 2020 collection, *Writing Democracy: The Political Turn In and Beyond the Trump Era*. This reinvigorated social turn—as scholars like Jacqueline Rhodes and Jonathan Alexander (2014) underline in a special issue of *College English*—continues the field's earlier social turn in the 1980s. An exchange of articles between Linda Flower and John Hayes and Patricia Bizzell during that time initiated the intellectual shift: Bizzell (1982, 223) famously critiqued Flower and Hayes's (1980) cognitivist model of the writing process for missing a "connection to social context." The "new" social turn, Rhodes and Alexander contend, extends Bizzell's prior interventions into the 20-teens and beyond in order to consider "deeply contextualized action and radical possibility for English studies in general and composition studies in particular" (2014, 486). As unpacked in this chapter, however, even before Rhodes and Alexander's essay, Black and ethnic studies scholars in the field like Carmen Kynard (2013) had comprehensively contested the disciplinary history that suggests composition and literacy studies' social turn began in the 1980s, reading that turn instead as a product of Black student protest in the 1920s.

Angela Haas and Michelle F. Eble more specifically understand the "new" social turn as a social *justice* turn that marks "a collective disciplinary redressing of social injustice sponsored by rhetorics and practices that infringe upon, neglect, withhold, and/or abolish human, non-human animal, and environmental rights" (2018, 5). This notion of the social justice turn parallels Carter et al.'s conception of the "political turn." The "political turn," Carter et al. write, calls for a deeper negotiation with "the public and pedagogical role of teachers" and a deliberate linking of our work as both scholars and teachers to the "insight and strength from historical struggles for social and economic justice in labor, civil rights, Black Power, women's rights, and national liberation struggles" (2019, 2).

Spotlighting these disciplinary trends does not intend to equate legitimate, antiracist, social justice–oriented scholarship with the extreme fetishization of racial violence embodied by Krug or Vitolo. Rather, it illumines a longstanding culture in academia broadly, and rhetoric, composition, and English studies specifically, whereby the repackaging of racial violence serves white logics and ways of knowing. The rhetoric of "turns" forwards these logics and remains how rhetoric and composition studies commonly understand its disciplinary history. The dominant and canonical history of the field as a discipline usually unfolds as follows: current-traditionalism in the late nineteenth to twentieth centuries, followed by the expressivist turn in the 1960s and 1970s, the cognitivist turn in the 1970s and 1980s, and the social constructionist turn from the 1980s onward. These turns lead finally to the post-process turn in the 1990s and 2000s and the "social justice turn" in the 2010s. Significantly, this history—which continues to be stressed in introductory-level graduate seminars and current scholarship, even when engaged critically—presents a *linear* narrative of (white) progress that begins with seemingly backward, problematic formalist/prescriptivist approaches to writing and moves slowly toward more political and culturally situated understandings of writing and literacy, as though Black, Indigenous, Latinx, and otherwise colonized peoples of color have not long understood writing and literacy as political and culturally situated. Such linear progressivism offers, at its crux, a white, imperialist logic. As Aníbal Quijano asserts, "linear, one-directional evolutionism from some [backward] state of nature to modern European society" typically characterizes colonial constructions of time (2000, 553). This phenomenon, Charles Mills (2014, 30, 31) reminds us, necessarily enables "amnesias, excisions, and forgettings" that position whiteness to master—and become master of—time. This manipulation of time functions as fertile means for benevolent gaslighting.

As this chapter illustrates, however, in addition to rhetoric, composition, and English studies' narration of its history through white progressivist logics, the field uses historic moments of racial/racist violences in the US throughout the twentieth century as motivation for its many "turns." This fetishizing and repackaging of racial pain and trauma as productive inspiration for white benevolence and "antiracism" grounds the operations of benevolent gaslighting as it proliferates in the academy. While this chapter explores this phenomenon across a range of humanities disciplines in the university, it focuses on the dominant threads of white, progressivist scholarship that help shape what rhetoric and composition studies terms its twenty-first-century "social justice" or "political" turn. It shows how the field's simultaneous upholding and invisibilizing of such scholarship's epistemologies and temporal logics can erase the ongoing antiracist theorizing, labor, and activism of Black, Indigenous, Latinx, and Asian/Asian-American scholars while concurrently enabling and justifying the seamless operations of the benevolent gaslight.

"Racial Forgetting/White Time" first unfurls how institutional mechanisms within and related to US higher education historically enacts "racial forgetting" through its treatment of violences against peoples of color as grounds to engage "difference." It then zooms in on rhetoric and writing studies to discuss how its field-shaping mechanisms—such as scholarship, editorial anthologies, and other pedagogical frames—build on this institutional background to forward the benevolent gaslight. Within these disciplinary contexts, the chapter then unpacks how recent field-wide "turns" fuel the erasures of peoples of color to center whiteness in supposedly equity-based progress, before ending with a look at how whiteness studies as an epistemological frame makes violences against people of color a gaslighting imperative.

US Higher Education and Racial Time

The positioning of racial violence and trauma as pedagogical fodder for white "teaching moments" invokes a version of white time somewhat unique to the neoliberal academy where universities routinely narrate "learning," a highly valuable institutional commodity, as a path to social and civic consciousness. Consider institutional diversity efforts following recent instances of anti-Black and anti-Asian violence in the US meant to "teach" white people about race and racism: Ohio State's 2020 "21-Day Anti-Racism Challenge" after Floyd's and Taylor's murders (Wexner Medical Center 2020); Washington University in St. Louis's "Day of Dialogue and Action" after the 2014 Ferguson Uprising (McCarthy 2020); or the University of Kansas's 2021 "listening and support conversations" in response to the 2021 anti-Asian Atlanta shootings (Graham et al. 2021). And in rhetoric and writing studies, a field itself centrally concerned with the transformative power of pedagogy, one might look to the CCCC "Statement on Violence at the Capitol on January 6, 2021" (2021). Again mobilizing teaching/learning as a response to racism, the statement "reaffirms our mission" as teachers to equip students "with the means to make sense of their worlds" and to "work toward healing" (CCCC 2021). While educating students about the violences of racism remains important, these discourses' positioning of individualized pedagogical practices as a path to a more just future risks structurally rescripting racial violences as material for (white and "universalized") learning.

These examples' fusing of antiracism with pedagogy invokes a particular temporality that white, progressive publics often embrace in their calls to "learn from the past" as a means to a better "future." As Ohio State's "21-Day Anti-Racism Challenge" states, "understanding, acknowledging, and relearning our American history of racism" serve as "a powerful lens" for "our journey to become anti-racists" (Wexner Medical Center 2020, n.p.). Here the challenge understands antiracism as a linear path that involves looking back *only* to move *forward*—a schema that leaves little room for racialized, nonlinear temporalities like anger and trauma that unsettle white futurity by being unable or unwilling to "get over it." The repetition of "our" furthers this process by forcing all readers into the same temporality: that is, "*our* journey to become anti-racists" (emphasis added). The repetition implies that if you are not part of "our journey," you will be left "behind" (in the racist past).

Whiteness's investment in forward, chronological movement casts Black, Indigenous, and peoples of color—as well as their histories of resistance, of culture-making, of imagining alternatives to colonial logics—as perpetually "in the past" (Quijano 2000, 553) while whites/Europeans are seen as "modern and futurally open" (Al-Saji 2013, 6). This renders colonized peoples' pasts "irrelevant to the present" (7) and, consequently, the future. However, white time also disavows *present* racism as a crucial element of its charge. As Alia Al-Saji advances in her reading of Fanon's *Black Skin, White Masks* (1952), white colonial frames not only naturalize racism—and specifically, anti-Blackness—but also *rationalizes* it as a "mere reaction to the racialized other" (2013, 4). This constitutes what Helen Ngo calls a "racialized forgetting" characterized by a "deliberate unknowing or not-knowing, but also a leaving behind and moving on" (2019, 234). Ngo points, for example, to how claims to innocence or ignorance typically deflect public controversies involving charges of racism (245). Paradoxically, these controversies often result in public declarations to "do better" in the future, yet continue to proliferate among white publics in repetitive and circular ways.

Krug's claims of both innocence via her "mental health demons" and exceptionalism through her assertion that she is "not like Shaun King or Rachel Dolezal" (even though she is, in practice, exactly like King and Dolezal) underscores the type of racial forgetting Ngo theorizes. In enacting these distancing moves, Krug decouples her racist acts from their racist history, which performs "a forgetting of racist histories" by recasting them as singular/exceptional instantiations (Ngo 2019, 245). Moreover, that Krug blames mental disability for causing her to claim a fake racial identity not only ascribes false agency to an imagined third party—mental health "demons"—but also embodies whiteness's continual ability "to move on from the [unsavory] past" by not having "to claim these pasts as one's own" (246). Racial forgetting, in effect, feeds benevolent gaslighting.

Racial forgetting, however, does more than campaign for white justification or erasure of the violences of past racist acts. Benevolent "antiracist" rhetorics often deploy it to imagine racial unity and resolution. Ngo, for example, in her analysis of "Australia Day," an Australian holiday meant to celebrate the declaration of British sovereignty on the land of the Gadigal peoples of the Eora nations, highlights two dominant narratives: the more conservative postracial rhetoric meant to urge Indigenous peoples to "get over" the histories of genocide and invasion the holiday commemorates; and a progressive postracial narrative mobilized by prime ministers, political leaders, and public organizations to rebrand the holiday as a generative opportunity for "national unity" and "coming together" (Ngo 2019, 248). Strikingly, the second vision of the holiday both implicitly acknowledges the historical violence of the event while at the same time imagining it as a basis for future learning, resolution, and societal/cultural growth.

The assumption that racist and colonial violences might be mobilized as groundwork for teaching white people about racism in hopes of redressing it acts as a brand of racialized forgetting foundational to contemporary US institutions of higher education in particular. Consider, for instance, the history of predominantly white US institutions of higher education and the post-WWII rise of diversity initiatives to

   RACIAL FORGETTING/WHITE TIME

appreciate the longstanding, insidious appeal of this narrative. As Jodi Melamed writes, a broader US imperialist project after the war motivated the institutionalization of literature in English Departments as an "efficacious tool for [white] Americans to get to know difference" (2011, 2), aiming to establish the country as a global geopolitical power in the twentieth century supposedly committed to racial and ethnic equality (20). A particular formation of racial liberalism that began in the 1930s inaugurated this impulse. Characterized by new alliances formed between Southern race liberals, Northern philanthropists, liberal sociologists, and African American intellectuals, the arrangement sought to address "the incapacity of New Deal programs to alleviate African American serfdom in the South" (18).

Interestingly, Melamed notes, many of the powerful Northern philanthropies involved in such initiatives and alliances worked largely in the field of education (i.e., the Carnegie Corporation, the Rockefeller Foundation, the Julius Rosenwald Foundation) in an effort to target Southern racial discrimination (18). These Northern philanthropies also "funded the rise of the liberal social sciences and thereby the dissemination of knowledges framing racial inequality through the rubric of the Negro problem" (18). In this way, philanthropy, as a largely white progressivist enterprise, "put its faith in social engineering, the idea that the gradual adjustment of white Southern beliefs and attitudes was the most effective method for improving racial conditions" (18).

Melamed specifically underscores the central importance of social scientific texts like Swedish economist Gunnar Myrdal's *An American Dilemma: The Negro Problem and Modern Democracy* (1944), commissioned by the Carnegie Corporation in 1937. For the two decades following its publication, *An American Dilemma* dominated popular and scientific discussions of race, ultimately becoming "an authoritative text within the disciplines of sociology, anthropology, and psychology" as well as "a guide for U.S. foreign policy" (Melamed 2011, 20). It fulfilled this latter purpose by characterizing "the Negro" as "America's Opportunity" to legitimate itself as a leader in the "decolonizing world," a campaign that "rhetorically linked liberal antiracism to U.S.

postwar global ascendancy in the register of nationalism and manifest destiny" (20), and—to put a finer point on it—rescripted violent histories of anti-Blackness as fodder for both white progressivism and US global dominance. This narrative, Melamed insightfully shares, ultimately recast racism as a *contradiction* to US liberal democratic ideals rather than—as history would suggest—deeply compatible with them. In so doing, it "valorized a set of altruistic Americanisms—abstract equality, individual rights, and market liberties—as the substantive content of antiracism" (20).

While Melamed's discussion of *An American Dilemma* provides important historical context for this phenomenon, similar (neo)liberal democratic narratives exist in contemporary whitestream and imperialist discourses surrounding writing and literacy. Since the 2010s, for example, US and Global North–based rhetorics surrounding writing and literacy-learning as a path to democracy specifically in the context of communities in the Global South have surged. Humanitarian, education-based nonprofits based in the Global North like Girl Rising state that they seek to use "the power of storytelling to change the way the world values girls and their education" ("Girl Rising" 2024). The organization links their efforts to increase "girls" in the Global South's access to education and literacy to normatively liberal-democratic, pro-capitalist ideals typically valorized in the Global North, often even framing "girls" themselves as a kind of global economic and sustainable resource ("Future Rising" 2024). Often narrated as key to addressing global inequality, this rhetoric portrays monolithically racialized girls from largely the Middle East, Africa, and Asia as "sites of [future] investment" (MacDonald 2016, 13), and thus closely parallels *An American Dilemma*'s characterization of US Black communities in the 1940s as "America's Opportunity" to legitimate itself as a world leader. Indeed, as many rhetoric, postcolonial, and cultural studies scholars highlight, US humanitarian outreach targeting "Third World" girls, as in *An American Dilemma*, works in intimate concert with Western imperialism, militarism, and expansion, especially in the post-9/11 context (Hesford 2011, Mohanty 1984, Sensoy and Marshall 2010).

These depoliticized and abstracted understandings of US democratic ideals and liberal-capitalist empowerment, in rescripting US democracy and its history as crucial to racial progress, reveal what Mills articulates as whiteness's "timelessness and racelessness" (2014, 32). The postracial and "altruistic" Americanisms that insidiously script US dominant political and economic frameworks as fundamentally antiracist or decolonial merge "postraciality . . . into preraciality, which is araciality, which is the abstract universal" (32). Put differently, Mills explains, "white time recapitulates the aspirational postracial future not just in the present but in the past," centering whiteness as "representative of the [universal] human condition" and fundamentally inclusive of all other races, even while still reflecting its original exclusionary practices (32). This rhetorical paradigm historically allowed—and continues to allow—linear progress narratives of white benevolence and normative recognition of peoples of color to function as seemingly universal, "relatable" entry points into "antiracist" political, economic, and educational initiatives. Rhetorics of white benevolence and saviorism in campaigns like Girl Rising reflect this pattern in invisibly, yet universally, upholding and idealizing whitestream US and Western notions of empowerment and transformation. Dominant approaches to teaching antiracism that often introduce discussions of race and racism through the works of *white* authors speaking from white subjective positionalities also uphold the trend. A quick search on Google Scholar, for example, reveals that the most-cited work on "white privilege" is white scholar Peggy McIntosh's "White Privilege: Unpacking the Invisible Knapsack" (1990). Similarly, in summer 2020, amid Black Lives Matter protests after Floyd's murder, the number-one best-selling book on both Amazon and *The New York Times* was white scholar Robin DiAngelo's 2018 book, *White Fragility: Why It's So Hard for White People to Talk About Racism* (Bergner 2020).

Despite the radical Civil Rights–era student activist movements and organizing that ultimately led to the mid-to-late-twentieth-century creation of critical race/ethnic studies programs like Black studies, Asian American studies, and Indigenous studies intended to center the works of racially and culturally minoritized scholars and activists,[3] US universities post–World War II and into the present have nonetheless become one of the most influential sites for "recalibrating" state interests. The pedagogical and curricular initiatives that accompanied this project, such as the deployment of "race novels" in English departments and literary studies to "teach tolerance," predominantly aimed, and largely *still* aim, toward white students' abstract engagements with racial difference rather than an emphasis on materialist "knowledge produced from below to create new horizons of social possibility" (Melamed 2011, 32). This political, economic, and cultural imperative, in claiming to socialize students as "multicultural subjects," commodifies racial difference and past racial violence within an abstract neo/liberal-multicultural framework of "identity, recognition, and representation" (96). Historically, these pedagogical initiatives, in the wake of the Civil Rights movement, have typically stayed within the bounds of a "master narrative" that emphasizes the linear triumphs of racial minorities—and specifically, African-Americans—in "defeating racism" through "full inclusion in American democracy" (37), even as anti-Blackness and xenophobia continued on behind the scenes post–Civil Rights in the form of Reagan-era initiatives to shrink welfare, the War on Drugs, the rise of privatized prisons,[4] and ongoing US state and military-sanctioned racial violence.

The dominant epistemological paradigm whereby racial progress both indirectly and directly hinges upon *white* recognition in the US and Global North plays a central role in the logics and operations of the benevolent gaslight. The futurally oriented progressivist ethos deployed by publics for racial domination across popular, cultural, and educational contexts repackages histories of racial violence and unrest as part of a past "we" can "finally" move beyond or overcome. Whiteness's benevolent rebranding of racial/racist pasts as opportunity for moral or political growth and learning endows it with a kind

---

3 See Ferguson (2012) for an expanded discussion of these histories as well as chapter 3, in which we discuss histories of student activism and organizing in greater length.
4 See Alexander (2010) and Hinton (2016).

of power to "dictate the pace of racial progress" (Cooper 2016, n.p.). This narrative, in turn, enables whiteness to both reassert its "temporal hegemony" (Carey 2020, 270) while at the same time reprising its positionality as universally "representative of the human condition" (Mills 2014, 32). As a result, peoples of color who might attempt to resist this paradigm by asserting our lived experiences of racialization might inevitably be cast as stuck in the past or resistant to "real" progress. Indeed, examples like public outrage in response to Black Lives Matter protesters' supposed violence and destruction of property to white suspicion toward so-called "cancel culture" aptly demonstrate this phenomenon.

White Progressivism in Rhetoric and Writing Studies

The benevolent gaslight's white progressivist temporality reasserts whiteness at the center of "social justice" while at the same time rendering its presence invisible. While Melamed foregrounds the complicity of English departments and literary studies in this temporal-epistemological paradigm, rhetoric and composition, more specifically, too, has long centered its own brand of white progressivism as a discipline that largely came of age in the postwar and Civil Rights eras through the 1970s process movement. As some historians of the field proffer, these historical contexts critically shaped the discipline (Kynard 2013, Parks 2000, Smitherman 2003). Much of the canonical scholarship and histories of the field, however, too often obscure and dematerialize these influences. Stephen Parks in *Class Politics* (2000), for instance, critiques the ways that white, progressivist proponents of the 1970s process turn reductively abstracted and dematerialized African-American histories and violences, often equating—as in the case of Ken Macrorie's *Uptaught* (1970)—African American liberation struggles to "an English student's quest for personal freedom" (Parks 2000, 76). Lisa Delpit similarly criticizes the process turn in the 1980s for its lack of a situated engagement with the specific lived realities of students and teachers of color. Teachers of color, she avers, often feel a sense of estrangement from white progressive process advocates when they might dismiss approaches to writing pedagogy deemed "too 'skills-oriented'" (Delpit 1988, 281). White liberalism works through this phenomenon to obscure its own whiteness (and, by extension, the privileges and power it affords). Because "those with power are frequently least aware of—or least willing to acknowledge—its existence," Delpit shows that the process movement's unequivocal rejection of explicit, prescriptive "rules" or expectations in favor of indirect, less structured writing pedagogy could sometimes result in further disenfranchising those always-already excluded from the white normative frames that nonetheless materially dictate one's access to dominant literacies and ways of knowing (284). Recalling Mills's observation about whiteness's appeals to abstract universality, both Parks and Delpit critique white progressive impulses in the field to universalize and abstract particular frameworks for writing pedagogy and instruction from their racialized materialities and histories.

These rhetorics' evacuation of the embodied, material, and historical specificities of race combined with their simultaneous reassertion of whiteness as epistemologically neutral or malleable sets the stage for the benevolent gaslight. Such logics, in turn, continue to enable a white, progressive ethos in the field to operate flexibly, universally, and even ahistorically—a framework that shapes rhetorics of racial identity, violences, and history through, as George Yancy (2017) underlines, a white gaze of innocence and purity. Racialized subjects and ways of knowing, then, necessarily function as objects "of the ethnographic gaze" (Yancy 2017, xvi) or—in the case of the benevolent gaslight, specifically—mechanisms for white antiracist learning or growth. One might consider, for instance, the field's continued use of aracial, monolithic terms like "student" or "writer" in its scholarship and disciplinary rhetorics when race or identity more broadly do *not* explicitly drive analytical focus. In these rhetorical situations, race typically does not figure meaningfully into analysis unless a discussion specifically *about* race arises as a site of study. Unless otherwise specified, this paradigm by default affixes whiteness as agent, nonwhiteness as object.

Additionally, the field of rhetoric and composition carries a distinctly complicated identity with often stated "revolutionary" goals while simultaneously deeply entrenched in institutional and state-serving interests via its involvement with university enrollments, professionalization, accreditation, and federal funding (Trimbur 2019, 34). This paradoxical position may perhaps explain why many moments of racial violence and disruption in the field's history have involved the sometimes contradictory leveraging of radical, moderate, and conservative interests, as well as the centering of a white progressive ethos committed to gradual—as opposed to radical—change. In reflecting on the drafting and legacy of CCCC/NCTE's 1974 "Students' Right to Their Own Language" (SRTOL), for example, Geneva Smitherman characterizes the final document ultimately endorsed by both organizations as, at its crux, a "compromise publication" (Smitherman 1995, 24) whose momentum emerged in part from Dr. King's 1968 assassination, which happened to occur at the same time as CCCC's 1968 convention. Even as Dr. King's assassination and the racial reckoning among white publics that followed solidified the fact that race functions as "a central component of linguistic difference" among dominant (white) circles in field (Smitherman 2003, 14), SRTOL's true legacy and history—which owes much to the Black Power movement, the Black Arts movement (BAM), and Civil Rights–era Black student protest movements (Kynard 2013)—stay underrecognized. As Kynard puts it, the radical possibilities of SRTOL in this way remain "always imagined and yet never fully achieved" as largely a result of the field's "inadequate responses" to the radical calls of 1960s Civil Rights and social justice movements—in particular, the consciousness-raising of Black Power (74).

One might easily find versions of these inadequate responses in the way canonical whitestream accounts of the discipline still often incompletely or reductively historicize SRTOL. For instance, Pritha encountered SRTOL for the first time in her professional career during the first-year writing teaching practicum when she began graduate school in 2013 as a graduate teaching associate. At that time, those directing the practicum presented SRTOL as merely a set of dehistoricized best-practices for teaching first-year international students, not as a result of nearly a century of radical antiracist organizing and intellectual knowledge-making. This common and misguided application of SRTOL suggests it as mostly relevant to the "other" located outside the national boundaries of the US—a framing that conveniently papers over other kinds of racial differences relevant to SRTOL to forward a national "we" (perhaps racialized as white) in the face of an international "them." This dialectic again recenters and naturalizes a benevolent, white progressivist pedagogical gaze that positions a white-representative "us" as the ultimate arbiters of antiracist, culturally responsive writing pedagogy. Such a narrative at once erases *and* capitalizes upon the historical race-radical literacies and Black resistance labor that made SRTOL possible in the first place. Yet again, the labors, traumas, and resistance work of peoples of color become fodder for dehistoricized, whitestream antiracist work.

Importantly, though, revisiting an argument Kynard forwards in her historicization of the central significance of Black student protests throughout the twentieth century might also make sense of the erasure and decontextualization of SRTOL's more radical origins: If one traces the epistemological and political interventions of landmark 1920s Black student protests that ultimately set the stage for the Civil Rights–era student protests of the 1950s and 1960s,[5] one might locate how what rhetoric and compositionists have come to understand as the "social turn"—whereby literacy became widely recognized and

---

5 In the 1920s, Black Fisk University students organized to protest the university's "supra-genteel dress code, requirements to sing old-time spirituals at Jim Crow concerts, and suppression of the campus newspaper" (Kynard 2013, 30). When no changes were made after student-faculty meetings, discussions, and demonstrations about these issues in November and December of 1924, students protested by breaking curfew, bum-rushing buildings, breaking windows, and overturning chairs (30). Student protesters successfully forced the university's white, male president, Fayette McKenzie, out of office by 1925. As Kynard notes, Black student protests like those at Fisk not only helped birth Black student protests in the 1950s and 1960s but also "fundamentally challenged the purposes and definitions of literacy" at the university and ruptured racialized and "fixed notions of learning according to dominant definitions of and relationships between institutions of power and racially subordinated [Black] masses" (33).

thought of as "a collaborative and socially interactive process"—began long before the 1980s genealogy underscored in dominant histories of the field (Kynard 2013, 33).

Kynard's work, in the context of this analysis, then, opposes the white temporal logics that underpin rhetoric and composition's "turns." Strikingly, disciplinary turns have historically only been recognized as turns when they have been initiated through the intellectual theorizing of progressive *white* scholars. Rhodes and Alexander's own reflection on the "new" social turn and the history that has informed it reinforces this perception. For them, Bizzell's critique of Flower and Hayes in the 1980s first enacts a "critical consciousness" and shift in "how many compositionists understood their work as teachers and scholars" (Rhodes and Alexander 2014, 483). Meanwhile, in their essay, they narrate the work of "compositionists studying race and ethnicity" as temporally *after* Bizzell's work as part of a "second shift" or "last turn to the social" (Rhodes and Alexander 2014, 484). This imaginary implicitly frames the embodied and epistemological labor of historical antiracist student protest movements—of Black scholars like Smitherman and Ernece Kelly, whose work foundationally shaped frameworks for linguistic justice in the 1970s,[6] and of Black Power and BAM artists and activists—as secondary (and temporally subsequent) to the groundbreaking intellectual reckonings of white scholars.

This dominant historical account of the field not only evinces a kind of racial forgetting but also articulates whiteness's historical tendency to temporally dictate the pace of social progress and "inclusion." Whiteness, Brittney Cooper contends, systematically displaces peoples of color through, for example, the theft of life via state-sanctioned racial violences, of space via gentrification, of personhood and humanity, of lost moments of joy, ultimately "urging complacency through endless calls to just be patient" (Cooper 2016, n.p.).[7] Having long-controlled

---

6 See Smitherman (2003) and Kynard (2013) for expanded discussions of both scholars' work in foundationally shaping frameworks for linguistic justice in relation to Black Power and the Black Arts movement (BAM).

7 In addition to the scholars cited throughout this essay (Al-Saji 2013; Mills 2014; Ngo 2019; Quijano 2000), see also King (1963) and Hartman (2002) for earlier

the narration and documentation of history, it has come to "own and master time" by deciding how and when race can "matter," and when it does not (Cooper 2016, n.p.). This system of "temporal hegemony," Tamika Carey writes, perpetually "pushes equity for a group further out of reach" (2020, 270) by implicitly or explicitly obscuring or even punishing those who assert agency in response to the logics and ideologies that disadvantage or erase them (284). Such hegemony works in concert with the implied benevolence of an inclusion-based white progressivism that has "finally" learned to "include" Black and otherwise racialized scholars' disciplinary knowledge-making labor temporally *after*, or in response to, moments of white erasure, violence, or racial unrest writ large. Rhodes and Alexander implicitly embrace this temporality in their discussion of the reimagined "latest" social turn, noting that recent "economic and material challenges" urge "a renewed and reinvigorated attention to . . . critiques that push us to consider more thoroughly issues of race and class" (2014, 486). Here Black peoples, Indigenous peoples, and peoples of color in the field already laboring for decades—building from a much more complex history and genealogy of Black and critical race and ethnic studies traditions in the field—might feel puzzled, or even *gaslit*, by their suggestion for "us" to renew and reinvigorate antiracist critiques. Have "we" not been here doing this work this whole time?

Other dominant histories of rhetoric and writing studies typically do not extensively recognize the foundational works of Black, Indigenous, Latinx, or Asian/Asian-American scholars (and students) in the field until the 1980s, and even then, they frequently only do so in the context of abstract discussions of postmodernism rather than radical antiracism or decoloniality. These histories also mirror the logics of Western expansion and colonialism. Not surprisingly—as Damían Baca (2008) illuminates in his analysis of Bizzell and Herzberg's massively popular anthology of the field, *The Rhetorical Tradition*

conversations about the racialization of time, history, and rhetorics of progress. Toni Morrison has also routinely explored the racial distortion and erasure of Black histories in her literary works, criticisms, and interviews (Davis and Morrison 1988).

(1990)—the works of scholars of color do not substantially appear until the sections on modernism and postmodernism. Such a temporality suggests scholars of color did not arrive to be "recover[ed]" (Bizzell and Herzberg 1990, iv) until a critical stage of twentieth-century Western/colonial development in North America; as such, these scholars and their contributions act as merely "an addendum to the looming historical progression of Westward expansion and assimilation" (Baca 2008, 153). This script, in turn, suggests race only comes to "matter" in a field's history when "discovered" by white Europeans. Furthermore, that Bizzell and Herzberg describe their second edition's inclusion of "more work by men and women of color and white women" as motivated by "new scholarship" in the field (2001, iv) denies the included Black and Latinx scholars (i.e., Henry Louis Gates Jr., Gloria Anzaldúa, Frederick Douglass) the capacity for importance on their own terms—instead, these scholars of color only become relevant as a result of "new scholarship" and normative (white) recognition.

The newly released 2020 edition of *The Rhetorical Tradition* does little to challenge the temporal narrative and disciplinary history of the earlier editions, even in spite of Bizzell, Herzberg, and new edition editor Robin Reames's more emphatic attempts to problematize the field's Eurocentrism and whiteness. Their editorial introduction explains that they divide "the historical development of rhetoric" into "four chronological periods": Ancient Rhetoric, Medieval and Renaissance Rhetoric, Modern Rhetoric, and Contemporary Rhetoric. They offer that "[t]hese divisions reflect the standard periodization applied to the history of ideas in the West but are admittedly arbitrary and have been adopted largely for convenience" (2020, 116). Save for passing references to a few Islamic orators and philosophers like al-Kindi, al-Farabi, Ibn-Sina, and Ibn-Rushd, their historical overview then proceeds to narrate the rhetorical contributions of largely Greco-Roman, European, and colonial cultures throughout history—from Aristotle to Cicero to Campbell—finally culminating in an overview of "contemporary" rhetorical turns, such as New Rhetoric (i.e., Burke, Weaver, Booth) and the linguistic and poststructuralist turns (Heidegger, Foucault, Derrida,

Habermas). The editors briefly identify scholars "examin[ing] the larger political consequences" of discourses of power as Anzaldúa, Gates, and Héléne Cixous (Bizzell et al. 2020, 145). In the Modern Rhetoric overview, they also claim that "the abolitionist movement also gave women and men of color, such as Maria Stewart and Frederick Douglass, a platform from which to make eloquent demands for human rights" (139). These rhetors' work, they add, preceded "a long process of democratization in American higher education" marked by the increased enrollments of "people of color and women" in colleges and universities (140). The racial inclusion logics at play here technologize the benevolent gaslight as both disciplinary and epistemological norm.

Like the 1990 version, the 2020 edition not only continues to fund the temporal logics of Western expansion and colonialism in the name of standardization and "convenience" but also presents the works of Black, Latinx, and Arab rhetors as enhancements or simple inclusions into the existing "arbitrary"/"convenient" canon. Both editions disappear rhetoricians of color as agents of original or foundational knowledge-making/remaking in rhetorical studies, instead making them visible only in terms of (1) their work in merely expanding understandings of the "political consequences" of still-preeminent Eurocentric thinking; (2) their resistance work *as a result of* "the abolitionist movement," which "gave" people of color "a platform"; or (3) their identity as *students* as a result of mere historical circumstances (i.e., "a long process of democratization in American higher education"). All three of these representations implicitly critique whitestream, Eurocentric thinkers and knowledge-making; yet whiteness and Eurocentricism nonetheless remain at the center of what constitutes pioneering rhetorical studies scholarship, even despite the volumes of scholarship by rhetoricians of color who both challenge the canon and articulate racially and culturally specific historical accounts and scholarly archives altogether. Take, for example, Kynard's abovementioned 2013 scholarship on the histories of Black activism in the nineteenth and twentieth centuries that fundamentally initiated the "long process of democratization in American higher education" to which Bizzell et al. (2020) ambiguously refer; or the Black Arts movement/Black Power–era race-radical literacies that fueled the linguistic turn (Kelly 1968, Kynard 2013, Smitherman 1977); or Gwendolyn Pough's groundbreaking scholarship on the Black public sphere (2004) that critically divests from the work of white poststructuralists like Habermas (prominently featured in Bizzell et al.'s 2020 collection). These omissions dissolve in a chronological, gaslighting charge where "inclusion" of Black and other racialized intellectualisms serve the rehabilitation (however understated) of a white-dominant disciplinary narrative.

Bizzell et al.'s elision of these works and/or their vague, passing references to them thus reinforce a "linear colonial history" that perpetually defers the "closed" or seemingly self-limiting histories of colonized peoples to "the open time of European modernity" (Al-Saji 2013, 7). While Bizzell et al. express discomfort with this linear colonial history when they identify it as arbitrary, that they nonetheless fail to delink their anthology from this history out of "convenience" articulates whiteness's presumed universality and openness (in opposition to, one might assume, the presumably "closed" or partial histories of colonized peoples). White, European history looms omniscient as all-encompassing, for *everyone*, while the histories of peoples of color function for *them*—inappropriate or "convenient" as framing for a broadscale disciplinary anthology. This schema, despite presented as critical of Western and colonial historical logics, still casts whiteness as epistemologically agential and infinitely flexible, naturalizing two integral conditions for the benevolent gaslight: (1) the antiracist intellectual and political labors of peoples of color become opportunity to repair or revise whiteness without unsettling or decentering it; and (2) white logics and histories self-represent as benevolent toward, or amenable to, peoples of color despite well-documented historical evidence to the contrary.

The Both/And of the "Political" and "Social Justice" Turns

With these points in mind, this chapter calls into question a history of rhetoric and composition that moves from formalism/current-traditionalism linearly toward seemingly more complex, progressive ways of engaging with questions of identity and difference, as though the social and political uses of literacy emerged unknown, unfelt, or unexperienced until the social turn in the latter part of the twentieth century. Whose history and whose scholarship does the dominant narration of the field's history make visible? Who, in the 1980s, perceived these realizations as "new"? As Kathleen Blake Yancey spotlights as recently as 2018, John Trimbur first coined the phrase "social turn" in the early 1990s in a piece in which he reviews three books that "represent literacy as an ideological arena and composing as a cultural activity" (Yancey 2018, 18). In continually repeating the marker of "social turn," which scholarship that followed then echoed, Yancey shares that Trimbur "provide[d] exigence for new scholarship" by enabling "a kind of interrogation of practice and theory" (20). Remarkably, Yancey does not interrogate this assertion much further, given that the phrase "provided exigence" reveals a troubling naturalization of white, male scholars as the nucleus for how to understand the discipline's history and formation. Further enforcing this calculus, Yancey instead asserts that shifts in cultural theory instigated by Paulo Freire and white, male Marxist critics such as Terry Eagleton and "streetwise literacy researchers such as Alan Luke" primarily motivated the social turn (17). These moves, then, further racially script said turn.

Given the historical and disciplinary developments in rhetoric, composition, and English studies throughout the twentieth century, how might one decouple the field's current social justice and political "turns" from the US white progressivist logics, temporalities, and ways of knowing that have long dominated it? Indeed, when Carter et al. introduce their theorization of the 2010s "political turn," they too seem critical of "turn" as a trope, highlighting their call for a political turn as not particularly new or novel (2019, 2). They state that much of the exigence behind the "political turn" project springs from "vibrant signs of political consciousness in pedagogical, theoretical, and activist insights in our field and across disciplines," with much of it "rooted in earlier, pioneering theory and critique, especially with respect to race, gender, indigeneity, and the painful legacy of Western colonialism, imperialism, and slavery (e.g., Combahee River Collective 1977, Condon and Young 2017, Horner et al. 2011, Ruiz and Sánchez 2016)" (Carter et al. 2019, 2). Ultimately, they contend that the political turn "underscores our view that the solutions to these escalating world problems will mean economic restructuring of global inequalities" intensified by capitalism and colonialism (2). They robustly consider the impacts of global neoliberal capitalism, as well as the many left-wing grassroots movements that emerged throughout the previous couple decades in response. Even as "we insist on our commitment to social justice," they continue, "our capacity to . . . help develop adequate responses to the crises occurring within and beyond the United States is attenuated by attacks on liberal democracy and the contradiction and corporatization of higher education" (7). They hold that because our disciplinary identity in rhetoric and composition "too often supersedes our role as politicized, public intellectuals," the field's radical critiques must move beyond the classroom and mere academic publication in order to ultimately become a field that "participates in *reclaiming* democracy" (7, 15). Despite Carter et al.'s legitimate call for work "that goes beyond theorizing" to more equitable public distribution and dissemination of the field's resources "in support of democratic deliberation and action" (15), the field must also do more to interrogate the racial implications of its own continual investment in "democratic deliberation," particularly along the lines of white progressivism and nationalism that inform the inherently racially-exclusionary meanings and wieldings of democratic ideals. Furthermore, how can rhetoric and writing scholars move "beyond theorizing" when often the field's dominant (white) patterns of theorizing themselves directly stranglehold its possibilities to "look to social movements for leadership and political insight" (15)?

Carter et al. embrace Marxist historical materialism in calling for scholars to follow the lead of social movements, a move which they suggest constitutes an "intersectional practice" that "provides an answer for America's failure to live up to its promises, whether to rectify economic inequality or to remedy racial, gender, and other forms of discrimination and oppression" (2019, 8). They believe this perspective uniquely enables a critical analysis of "larger theoretical themes and political struggles, such as the extrajudicial murders of [B]lack people, the 'New Jim Crow' of post–Civil War forms of [B]lack servitude, terrorization, and mass incarceration, and the Black Lives Matter movement and other forms of struggle to end them" (8). Indeed, many groundbreaking Black feminist and queer of color critique scholars actively challenge Marxist historical materialism's capacity for comprehensively making visible the co-constitutiveness of race, gender, sexuality, and class given its long legacy of privileging class over other social relations (Combahee River Collective 1977, Ferguson 2003, Reddy 1998). Carter et al. underscore some of these critiques, drawing on Fanon's claims that "Marxist analysis should always be slightly stretched every time we have to do with the colonial problem" (2019, 40) and Cedric Robinson's (1983) work on the co-evolution of capitalism and racism. However, despite their cautionary note about the historical and epistemological partiality of Marxism, Carter et al. ultimately conclude that Marxism nonetheless "provides for us a way of thinking about the world in relation to twentieth- and twenty-first-century anti-colonial, anti-racist, anti-sexist, heteronormative, environmental, class struggles, and the specific work we must undertake" (2019, 10). Regardless of their important acknowledgment of some of Marxism's limitations, their ultimate suggestion that Marxist historical materialism stands amenable to "intersectional practice," without any discussion of the dehumanizing impacts of abstracting Black feminist frameworks like intersectionality from their roots in *specifically* Black feminist organizing and resistance, remains troubling. However, this erasure underscores again a question of crucial importance to this project: Why does whiteness—and the work of celebrated white scholars, thinkers, and activists like Marx—continue to operate as a flexible or universal frame for radical social justice work *even when* white scholars recognize the limitations and critiques of his work?

Rather than to minimize Marx's legacy and the important work of historical materialism, this question attends to why Marx and other Eurocentric scholars remain—both temporally and epistemologically—universal starting points for "thinking about the world in relation to twentieth- and twenty-first-century anti-colonial, anti-racist, anti-sexist, heteronormative, environmental, class struggles" (Carter et al. 2019, 10). This issue does not exist in unique relation to Marxism. On the contrary, it persists as a deeply entrenched phenomenon in rhetoric and writing studies (and the humanities more broadly) that the field has yet to comprehensively unsettle. The continual centering of classical and (neo)Aristotelian frameworks in the writing classroom as a starting point for teaching about rhetoric evidences this trend, along with the ongoing celebration of Kenneth Burke's "parlor" as a metaphor for rhetorical criticism, and the enduring efforts in rhetorical studies and beyond to cite and recover the scholarship of theorists like Martin Heidegger despite his documented ties to Nazism.[8] The theoretical, political, and epistemological flexibility continually and unevenly applied to the works of white, largely male theorists fuels the infinite bending of white logics toward a range of articulations of white dominance—from supremacy, to progressivism, to historical revisionism, to benevolent antiracism.

While one chapter cannot possibly trace the implications of all of these trends in rhetoric and composition's whitestream scholarship, the final section focuses briefly on an especially visible trend in the field that emerged throughout the last two decades' "social justice"

---

8 See Rockmore (1997) and Wolin (2023) for more on Heidegger's relationship to Nazism, particularly via his "Black Notebooks," which were published in 2014. While work in rhetoric and writing studies often cites Heidegger, his work has been particularly relevant to recent new materialist scholarship, such as that of Hawk (2018) and Rickert (2013). *The Rhetorical Tradition*'s 2020 edition, too, identifies Heidegger as foundational to rhetorical studies' linguistic turn without mentioning his Nazi ties. While Rickert, importantly, does acknowledge Heidegger's "problematic politics" (2013, 274), this discussion is not featured prominently until the book's conclusion.

turn: whiteness studies. The analysis therein does not suggest that whiteness studies–oriented rhetoric and writing studies are solely responsible for racialized epistemological violence in the discipline but rather that they illustrate more deeply how white progressivist theoretical frameworks in the wake of Ferguson and other hypervisible racial violences continue to rebrand racial violences as progressive, whiteness-centered "antiracist" opportunities in ways that risk compounding violence and erasure upon Black peoples, Indigenous peoples, and peoples of color. In short, it unpacks whiteness studies' entanglements with the benevolent gaslight.

Whiteness Studies

In *White Fragility* (2018), Robin DiAngelo proposes that making whiteness visible shifts "the locus of change onto white people, where it belongs. It . . . points us [white people] in the direction of the lifelong work that is uniquely ours" (33). She locates the project's exigence as motivated in part by both her personal reflections on her own racism as well as her experiences of being a diversity educator for "primarily white audiences" (2). Because of the "many brilliant and patient mentors of color" who helped her see how racism works, she "receive[d] feedback on [her] problematic racial patterns as a helpful way to support [her] learning and growth" (4). DiAngelo goes on to outline and expand on her theory of white fragility, which she identifies as a white progressivist impulse "triggered by discomfort and anxiety" to "reinstate white equilibrium" and racial comfort in situations where "good, moral" whites are called out for their complicity with racism (2). White fragility does not articulate weakness or vulnerability but instead emerges from "superiority and entitlement"; it functions as "a powerful means of white racial control and the protection of white advantage" (2).

In October 2019, Pritha witnessed DiAngelo deliver a public lecture at the University of Kansas. She attended the talk with her friend Brandon, a Black faculty member in the School of Public Affairs. Pritha and Brandon represented just a handful of peoples of color in the packed, mostly white audience. As DiAngelo began, she warned the audience that she would mention her whiteness and their whiteness hundreds of times in the talk. "It will be uncomfortable," she claimed, because white people don't like to talk about whiteness. At one point, DiAngelo listed all of her white privileges. After she read her list, she prompted audience members to turn to each other and engage in the same activity—the exercise assuming, perhaps, that privilege characterized everyone in the audience's relationship to race. The awkwardness that arose when Brandon and Pritha could not participate in this activity—like the white audience members who surrounded them—highlighted that DiAngelo did not design or intend the talk for an audience of people of color. The space DiAngelo had created in her relentless confrontation of whiteness had paradoxically opened up a kind of racism of its own, precisely in *recentering* whiteness. Not only did this conversation about racism uninvite people of color, but its logics themselves imagined people of color as absent/silent. Moreover, DiAngelo also stated at the beginning of the talk that it would not feature a Q&A segment after her presentation. Though possibly a tactic to prevent white audience members from making offensive remarks, it also silenced any people of color in the audience with potential feedback or legitimate questions about DiAngelo's work and her approach.

This scene from DiAngelo's talk emphasizes some of the central material, temporal, and epistemological issues of popular whiteness studies–based approaches to antiracism. First, in imagining white people as antiracism's primary audience—in much the same way Gries's apology letter does in the introductory chapter—approaches like DiAngelo's reinforce whiteness at the center of antiracist work while also alienating and even erasing historical and ongoing resistance work of peoples of color who have long raised and addressed these very same questions about white privilege (Maraj 2020). Second, and perhaps most importantly for this project, such approaches rely upon a retroactive temporality of injury-response rather than a *proactive* temporality of prevention-resistance. DiAngelo's early suggestion in her book that the "feedback" she received about her "problematic racial patterns" from her "brilliant and patient mentors of color" who "supported [her] learning and growth" illustrates these dynamics (2018, 4). In suggesting that DiAngelo's own learned racism as a white woman ultimately led her to become an acclaimed antiracism and diversity educator, she enacts a version of the benevolent gaslight: She casts her "mentors of color" who helped her learn about racism as patient, unconditional educators for white learning rather than as potential early recipients of DiAngelo's racisms who may very well have been educating her as a way of advocating for their own personhood. DiAngelo understands this work, though, not as *resistance* to whiteness, but as generosity toward it.

The historical contexts arguably responsible for propelling the work of public intellectuals and whiteness studies scholars like DiAngelo into the spotlight also proves revealing. Though published in 2018, *White Fragility* rose to the top of *The New York Times* and Amazon's best-seller lists only after Floyd's murder and subsequent protests. Major corporations like Nike, Under Armour, Goldman Sachs, Facebook, and CVS then called on DiAngelo to deliver high-profile antiracism workshops; she appeared on Jimmy Fallon's show, and her book populated antiracism reading lists across popular media channels (Bergner 2020). In other words, a high-profile act of state-sanctioned anti-Black violence largely premised and motivated her popular success as a scholar and public intellectual. What makes the recognition of whiteness and its impacts so often temporally and materially contingent upon racial injury and trauma to Black people, Indigenous people, and people of color? Whose bodies, whose resistance work, and whose scholarship become invisible when the racist injury and trauma to Black people, Indigenous people, and peoples of color primarily fuels white progressive reckoning and introspection? When acts of racial domination operate as pedagogy for whiteness to overcome its own violence—as in dominant whiteness studies work like DiAngelo's—these dynamics deem the existence of those racialized as not only perpetually violable but also primarily visible in moments of *white* violence or recognition. This arrangement funds the inherent race-making of the benevolent gaslight.

RACIAL FORGETTING/WHITE TIME

Over the past two decades, critical race studies work that centrally interrogates whiteness—both that which explicitly identifies itself as whiteness studies and that which does not—rose to immense recognition and popularity in rhetoric and writing studies. One might think of Krista Ratcliffe's now canonical work, *Rhetorical Listening: Identification, Gender, Whiteness* (2005), Wendy Ryden and Ian Marshall's *Reading, Writing, and the Rhetorics of Whiteness* (2013), Tammie M. Kennedy, Joyce Irene Middleton, and Krista Ratcliffe's "The Matter of Whiteness: Or, Why Whiteness Studies Is Important to Rhetoric and Composition" (2005), and the 2018 CCCC Outstanding Book Award (Edited Collection) winner, *Rhetorics of Whiteness: Postracial Hauntings in Popular Culture, Social Media, and Education* (2017) edited by Kennedy, Middleton, and Ratcliffe. Other related scholarship includes work from writing program administration studies, such as Asao B. Inoue's influential interrogation of the "white racial habitus" that characterizes hegemonic approaches to writing pedagogy and assessment, a theory he outlines in his 2017 CCCC Outstanding Book Award-winning *Antiracist Writing Assessment Ecologies* (2015).

In their 2005 essay, Kennedy et al. provide a robust overview of whiteness studies and its history. They begin by rightly crediting Toni Morrison for initially bringing whiteness studies to the attention of English studies in 1992 with her groundbreaking work, *Playing in the Dark: Whiteness and the Literary Imagination.* They outline whiteness studies as a corollary of critical race studies, which seeks to "critique race and whiteness as they play out, paradoxically through visibility and invisibility, in US culture" (Kennedy et al. 2005, 361). These scholars highlight Patricia Williams's *The Alchemy of Race and Rights* (1991) and Kimberlé Crenshaw et al.'s *Critical Race Theory: The Key Writings That Formed the Movement* (1995) as other formative works. Indeed, while whiteness studies work has significantly impacted understanding of the systematic and coded nature of race/racism, both Kennedy et al. and Ryden and Marshall do spotlight the limitations of whiteness-based approaches to antiracist work. Because whiteness studies can reify "the category of whiteness in a way that rechannels money and attention to white folks" (Kennedy et al. 2005, 362), they acknowledge that it risks recentering "the white subject by paying attention to the particularity of whiteness in its various incarnations" at the expense of a more situated and complex understanding of race (Ryden and Marshall 2013, 5). Despite the ways this work makes possible a deeper understanding of how public white supremacist energy leads to "dangerous consequences for our classroom and institutional spaces" (Maraj 2020, 10), "starting with whiteness and its undoing as the basis for antiracist agency" constitutes a deeply *reactive* approach rather than a *proactive* one (14). If the field's supposed twenty-first-century surge in "antiracist" attention "primarily strive[s] to repair whiteness or white cultures" (14), it misses opportunities to spotlight "Black people and their antiracist energies" (10).[9] In the frame of dominant whiteness studies frameworks, however, those energies—as the case with DiAngelo—*could* exist as capital financing discussions of whiteness's workings.

To demonstrate further: Key differences separate a project such as Gries's Swastika Monitor project (2018)—which maps the public circulation of racist symbols and is discussed at length elsewhere (Prasad and Maraj 2022)—and the Black feminist and queer-centered organizing of Movement for Black Lives/Black Lives Matter. The latter movement propounds an *affirmation* of Blackness as opposed the former's emphasis on mapping articulations of white supremacy as a starting point for antiracism. Racist iconography like swastikas indeed might carry agency in shaping racialized subjects' embodied engagements with geographic spaces. However, Gries's approach centers racial violence (and symbols thereof) at the expense of a critical engagement with the embodied and spatialized forms of resistance mobilized both collectively and individually by Black people, Indigenous people, and people of color themselves. That project, thus, frames whiteness and white violence as *the* primary agent (Wright 2015, 116), thereby framing the actions of Black activists as perpetual *reactions* (47). In spite of Gries's mapping project's potential ambition or utility, it charts a geography exclusively legible through

---

9 See also Maraj (2022).

symbols of whiteness, ceasing ultimately to unhinge space "from the limiting demands of colonialism, practices of domination, and human objectification" (McKittrick 2006, 17). As a result, it also renders invisible Black "geographic alternatives" (17) and material practices of resistance that, as Black feminist scholar Katherine McKittrick (2006) argues, historically work "alongside and across traditional geographies" (xiv). Racial difference, then, subsumes in a narrative animated primarily by invisible (assumed racialized) victims, leaving them only agential in the intrinsic (goodly) ethos of white antiracism.

Organizational and professional initiatives in rhetoric and writing studies have accompanied the popularity of whiteness studies and whiteness studies–adjacent scholarship over the past few decades. Within the field, the CCCC/NCTE Task Force on Assessing Whiteness for Equity, Understanding, and Change within CCCC/NCTE formed in 2020. Consisting of five white scholars as of 2024—Frankie Condon (co-chair), Mara Lee Grayson (co-chair), Clare Bermingham, Cheryl Glenn, and Doug Kern—the task force assesses "the operation of white privilege, whiteliness, and whiteness within CCCC and NCTE"; identifies any "'unwritten rules' that have a disparate impact on minorities, and that may intentionally or unwittingly buttress white privilege;" and "consult[s] with other members of all backgrounds listening to their concerns and feedback" (Condon 2020). Notably, this task force also emerged on the heels of parallel efforts in rhetoric and communication studies via a #RhetoricSoWhite/#CommunicationSoWhite protest on Twitter that subsequently led to the publication of special issues, inspired #RhetoricSoWhite–themed antiracist workshops, and increased efforts within the Rhetoric Society of America and the National Communication Association to promote racial diversity within the discipline.[10] The trend of mobilizing "antiracist" action

---

10 In June 2019, Marty Medhurst, a Distinguished Scholar and the editor of *Rhetoric and Public Affairs*, wrote an editorial decrying recent initiatives to prioritize "diverse" scholars for publications and awards, which he claimed were a threat to intellectual merit. Medhurst was widely criticized among rhetoric and communication studies scholars and on social media under the hashtags #RhetoricSoWhite and #CommunicationSoWhite ("2019 #Communicationsowhite Controversy" 2019).

sparked by pervasive whiteness thus sustains in disciplinary and disciplinary-proximate spaces.

Though important work, the creation of an all-white CCCC/NCTE Task Force meant to assess whiteness in the discipline as a reaction to ongoing anti-Black and racist violence strikes as a curious—and potentially redundant—development in light of the field's extensive history of antiracist organizing among its Black, Latinx, American Indian, and Asian/Asian-American Caucuses. As Mariana Davis writes in her 1994 history of the Black Caucus, a series of unofficial meetings at CCCC and NCTE conventions in the late 1960s meant precisely to address the centering of whiteness in the discipline and the absence of Black scholars and teachers from convention programs motivated that Caucus's inception. The Black Caucus's work began with drafting resolutions presented to NCTE decision-making bodies in the 1960s (1994, 6), and this work has indeed continued on into the present. The Latinx, American Indian, and Asian/Asian American Caucuses have forwarded similar and parallel efforts, from the historical activisms of Chicanx writer Felipe de Ortego y Gasca that helped lead to the formation of the Latinx Caucus (García et al. 2019), to organizing among Asian-American scholars like LuMing Mao and Morris Young to establish the Asian/Asian-American Caucus (Sano-Franchini et al. 2017), to Malea Powell and Scott Lyons's efforts in the 1990s to form the American Indian Caucus (Anderson 2008). Through their ongoing organizing, these caucuses have continued work over the past several decades, both separately and coalitionally, to contest CCCC/NCTE's inaction in addressing racial violence in the discipline.[11] What impacts, then, do institu-

---

11 In addition to the caucuses' open letter to Gries in response to the incident at the 2018 Watson Conference, discussed in the introductory chapter, the caucuses also recently organized to contest the 2018 CCCC conference location of Kansas City, Missouri, in the wake of an NAACP travel advisory warning people of color not to travel to Missouri due to recent racial hate crimes and the passage of Missouri Senate Bill 43. SB 43 makes discrimination particularly hard to prove "by placing the burden of proof on the plaintiff to claim that race discrimination serves as a 'motivating' vs. 'contributing' factor" (García et al. 2019, 117). In response, the CCCC Latinx Caucus drafted a statement that eventually became a Joint Caucus Statement requesting a change to the conference location signed by the Black Caucus, the Asian/Asian American Caucus, and the American Indian Caucus (117).

tional efforts underscoring the need to specifically address whiteness via white frames produce?

Given nearly half a century of this scholarship, policy work, and ongoing organizing among scholars of color, the "unwritten rules" that disparately impact Black, Indigenous, Latinx, and Asian/Asian-American scholars and teachers in the field remain, in fact, already well known and felt. What invisible operations of whiteness in the discipline persist unrevealed? Or, rather, has the labor of Black, Indigenous, Latinx, and Asian/Asian-American scholars—who have robustly interrogated the field's historical racism—too often been devalued as individualistic, partial, or lacking rigor,[12] all while still systematically excluded from recognition from the field's dominant "turns"? The notion of whiteliness as "an articulation of epistemologies that have been racialized" (Condon 2011, 3) might help white scholars looking to better understand the implicit and explicit operations of whiteness. But what does it suggest when our professional organizations entrust white scholars to address whiteliness even though scholars of color have already been doing this critical work for a long time? Perhaps a version of racial forgetting (Ngo 2019, 234) operates—in this case, as prevalently elsewhere in the field—to master time (Mills 2014, 31)? Perhaps the benevolent gaslight runs deep in disciplinary spaces and thinking?

While whiteness studies and whiteness-based approaches to antiracism maintain their innately necessary significance to the field, the *temporal* elements at play in their deployment demands attention. Building from extant scholarship on racialized time (Al-Saji 2013; Mills 2014; Ngo 2019; Quijano 2000; Wright 2015) and that which

---

12 See Cushman et al. (2021) and Hidalgo (2021) for a recent debate surrounding cultural rhetorics scholarship's usage of counterstory as a decolonial methodology to challenge master (white) narratives. Cushman et al. argue—reductively, as Hidalgo highlights (Hidalgo 2021, 11)—that counterstory is inherently limiting as in its deployment by "self-identifying" representatives "of an oppressed or disenfranchised social group . . . who 'self-authorize' themselves as knowledge makers" (Cushman et al. 2021, 12). As Aja Martinez rightly notes in her book-length exploration of counterstory as critical race methodology, however, the suggestion of counterstory's use of personal narrative as limiting is misguided; rather than being merely individualistic, counterstory radically makes possible indispensable "additional truths" about the lived realities and materiality of race/racism (2020, 17).

questions the charge of whiteness as epistemological center of race work in rhetorical studies (Maraj 2020; Maraj 2022; Washington 2020), this chapter questions the temporality of whiteness-oriented work on three intersecting planes: (1) the reactive temporality often mobilized epistemologically within it; (2) the historical moments that materially spark critical and popular interest in such work; and (3) the erasures that often result from its approaches. All three temporal frames position whiteness as the intended recipient and benevolent agent of antiracism—as in the racialized assumptions that lead to DiAngelo's alienation of the people of color in her audience—while also hinging white progress, in so many ways, upon erasure, violence, and trauma to people of color. In so doing, white progressives, through their own past violences and their efforts to "do better" and forward "understanding" and "change" (recalling the NCTE/CCCC task force's title of "Assessing Whiteness for Equity, Understanding, and Change"), make claim to antiracist ethos, in spite of the ongoing pedagogical and resistance labor of the peoples of color who surround them. This logic rests on racist violence as both learning and *teaching* opportunity for whiteness, (race-)making it difficult to imagine a framework for justice-minded work independent of white recognition and inclusion when whiteness narrates as trader and/or audience of such goods.

Conclusion: From White Temporal Logics to the Benevolent Gaslight

In January 2021, Pritha presents an early version of this chapter in a panel on "Revisionist Histories" at the Modern Languages Association conference, occurring virtually due to the pandemic. On concluding her talk, she opens the Zoom chat window to read the comments attendees posted during it. One comment posted by a senior white woman faculty member causes her to do a double take: "Thank you for reminding us of the importance of this work." Perhaps it sparks an overreaction, but the use of the word "reminding" causes Pritha to spiral: *Wait, does this scholarship already exist? Am I rehashing an argument everyone already knows? Is there a book about this I haven't read?* These questions linger for a couple days after the conference.

At first, the irony of this self-doubt in the context of a project on benevolent gaslighting eludes Pritha. (That's how gaslighting works.) After all, she just delivered a whole research presentation—an entirely structured and comprehensively historicized argument from a project already under advance contract—about white temporal logics in the field's "social justice" scholarship. She quite literally argues that these white temporal logics have *not* yet been adequately recognized or challenged; no, this clearly isn't an argument everyone already knows. A couple more days pass, and Pritha finally realizes that this white woman's use of "reminding" itself ironically iterates the white temporal logic that principally concerns this project. By using "reminding," she posits an exceptionalized appeal to a particular ethos—the assumption being that she, a white woman, may *already* be positioned, and has long been positioned, toward antiracism. Perhaps more insidiously, though, "reminding" here also becomes a way of managing time and history such that it implies a woman of color junior faculty's intellectual work derivative, in the past—a suggestion that, Quijano might remind us, intrinsically invokes white, colonial time (2000, 553). "Reminding," in other words, acts as a racialized microaggression disguised as antiracism, born of a culture of academic whiteness that too often apprehends racial "progress" as *white* acknowledgment.

—

US institutions of education have long celebrated public figures and historical-literary texts that position white subjects as *antiracist* pedagogues, particularly as a response to ongoing and historical moments of racialized violence. In addition to the examples highlighted in this chapter, consider the nearly decades-long emphasis in secondary education English and language arts courses on celebrated texts like *To Kill a Mockingbird* (Lee 1960) and *The Adventures of Huckleberry Finn* (Twain 1884), "classic" novels that, in focusing on the racial reckonings of benevolent white male protagonists, have introduced children and adolescents to the history of racism in the US for decades. Unsurprisingly, critical reflections on race and racism across political, educational, and cultural institutions continue to mobilize a distinctly *white* gaze and reactive temporality.

As this chapter suggests, the fact that white theorists continue to dictate the pace of social progress (Cooper 2016) in political and social justice work in the humanities broadly—and in rhetoric and writing studies specifically—looms larger than citational or genealogical erasure. The conceptual and political flexibility applied in dominant readings of white scholars like Marx, Burke, and Heidegger crucially parallels the moral and ethical elasticity typically ascribed to whites whose past racist missteps or erasures have been repackaged to forward antiracist pedagogical ethos, as illustrated in this chapter's read of DiAngelo. The retroactive pliability of benevolent whiteness and its distinct capacities at "management of memory" (Mills 2007, 28) enable whiteness to renegotiate the past—and to benevolently *gaslight*—through a particular performance of "futurally-open" (Al-Saji 2013, 6) progressivism and a perpetually deferred antiracist future. Too often reductively understood as *white* recognition, "racial progress" in this frame ultimately positions colonized and racialized peoples as object lessons forever prostrate.

References

Alexander, Michelle. 2010. *The New Jim Crow: Mass Incarceration in the Age of Colorblindness*. New York: New Press.

Al-Saji, Alia. 2013. "Too Late: Racialized Time and the Closure of the Past." *Insights* 6 (5): 1–13.

Anderson, Joyce Rain. 2008. "Words to Speak: The American Indian Caucus at CCCC." *Reflections Journal* 8 (1): 251–257.

Anonymous. 2020. "CV Vitolo 'Haddad': Another Academic Racial Fraud?" Medium, September 4. https://medium.com/@polite_keppel_dinosaur_57/cv-vitolo-haddad-another-academic-racial-fraud-c5c41fe32110.

Baca, D. 2008. *Mestiz@ Scripts, Digital Migrations, and the Territories of Writing*. New York: Springer.

Bergner, Daniel. 2020. " 'White Fragility' Is Everywhere. But Does Antiracism Training Work?" *New York Times*, August 6. https://www.nytimes.com/2020/07/15/magazine/white-fragility-robin-diangelo.html.

Bizzell, Patricia. 1982. "Cognition, Convention, and Certainty: What We Need to Know About Writing." *PRE/TEXT* 3 (3): 213–244.

Bizzell, Patricia, and Bruce Herzberg, eds. 1990. The Rhetorical Tradition: Readings from Classical Times to the Present, 1st ed. New York: Bedford/St. Martin's.

Bizzell, Patricia, and Bruce Herzberg, eds. 2001. *The Rhetorical Tradition: Readings from Classical Times to the Present*, 2nd ed. New York: Bedford/St. Martin's.

Bizzell, Patricia, Bruce Herzberg, and Robin Reames, eds. 2020. *The Rhetorical Tradition: Readings from Classical Times to the Present*, 3rd ed. New York: Bedford/St. Martin's.

Carey, Tamika L. 2020. "Necessary Adjustments: Black Women's Rhetorical Impatience." *Rhetoric Review* 39 (3): 269–286. https://doi.org/10.1080/07350198.2020.1764745.

Carter, Shannon, Deborah Mutnick, Stephen Parks, and Jessica Pauszek, eds. 2019. *Writing Democracy: The Political Turn In and Beyond the Trump Era*. New York: Routledge.

Combahee River Collective. 1977. "Combahee River Collective Statement." *Internet Archive*. Accessed July 19, 2024. https://archive.org/details/Combahee1979.

Condon, Frankie. 2011. "A Place Where There Isn't Any Trouble." In *Code-Meshing as World English*, edited by Vershawn Ashanti Young and Aja Y. Martinez, 1–8. Urbana, IL: National Council of Teachers of English.

Condon, Frankie. 2020. "Report to CCCC Executive Committee: Taskforce on Assessing Whiteness for Equity, Understanding, and Change." October 19. Conference on College Composition and Communication. https://cccc.ncte.org/wp-content/uploads/2022/02/TF_Assessing_WhitenessNov2020.pdf.

Condon, Frankie, and Vershawn Ashanti Young, eds. 2017. *Performing Antiracist Pedagogy in Rhetoric, Writing, and Communication*. Denver: WAC Clearinghouse.

Conference on College Composition and Communication (CCCC). 2021. "Statement on Violence at the Capitol on January 6, 2021." https://cccc.ncte.org/cccc/cccc-statement-on-violence-at-the-capitol.

Cooper, Brittney C. 2016. "The Racial Politics of Time." TED Talk, February 21. https://www.ted.com/talks/brittney_cooper_the_racial_politics_of_time/transcript.

Cushman, Ellen, Damián Baca, and Romeo García. 2021. "Introduction: Delinking: Toward Pluriversal Rhetorics." *College English* 84 (1): 7–32. https://doi.org/10.58680/ce202131450.

Crenshaw, Kimberlé, Neil Gotanda, Gary Peller, and Kendall Thomas, eds. 1995. *Critical Race Theory: The Key Writings That Formed the Movement*. New York: New Press.

Davis, Christina, and Toni Morrison. 1988. "Interview with Toni Morrison." *Présence Africaine*, no. 145, 141–150.

Davis, Marianna W. 1994. *History of the Black Caucus of the National Council of Teachers of English*. Philadelphia: New City Community Press.

Delpit, Lisa. 1988. "The Silenced Dialogue: Power and Pedagogy in Educating Other People's Children." *Harvard Educational Review* 58 (3): 280–299. https://doi.org/10.17763/haer.58.3.c43481778r528qw4.

DiAngelo, Robin. 2018. *White Fragility: Why It's So Hard for White People to Talk About Racism*. Boston: Beacon Press.

Fanon, Frantz. 1952. *Black Skin, White Masks*. London: Pluto Press.

Ferguson, Roderick A. 2003. *Aberrations in Black: Toward a Queer of Color Critique*. Minneapolis: University of Minnesota Press.

Ferguson, Roderick A. 2012. *The Reorder of Things: The University and Its Pedagogies of Minority Difference*. Minneapolis: University of Minnesota Press.

Flower, Linda, and John R. Hayes. 1980. "The Cognition of Discovery: Defining a Rhetorical Problem." *College Composition and Communication* 31 (1): 21–32.

"Future Rising." 2024. GirlRising.org. https://www.girlrising.org/future-rising.

García, Romeo, Iris D. Ruiz, Anita Hernández, and María Paz Carvajal Regidor, eds. 2019. *Viva Nuestro Caucus: Rewriting the Forgotten Pages of Our Caucus*. Anderson, SC: Parlor Press.

"Girl Rising." 2024. GirlRising.org. https://www.girlrising.org/.

Graham, D. A., Derek Kwan, and Charles A. S. Bankart. 2021. "RE: Additional AAAPI Listening Sessions Scheduled for Thursday." Email to Pritha Prasad, April 19, 2021.

Grande, Sandy. 2003. "Whitestream Feminism and the Colonialist Project: A Review of Contemporary Feminist Pedagogy and Praxis." *Educational Theory* 53 (3): 329–346. https://doi.org/10.1111/j.1741-5446.2003.00329.x.

Gries, Laurie. 2018. "Swastika Monitoring: Developing Digital Research Tools to Track Visual Rhetorics of Hate." In *Making Future Matters*, edited by Rick Wysocki and Mary P. Sheridon. Computers and Composition Digital Press. https://ccdigitalpress.org/book/makingfuturematters/gries-part-3.html.

Haas, Angela M., and Michelle F. Eble. 2018. "Introduction: The Social Justice Turn." In Key Theoretical Frameworks: Teaching Technical Communication in the Twenty-First Century, edited by Angela M. Haas and Michelle F. Eble, 3–19. Logan: Utah State University Press.

Hartman, Saidiya. 2002. "The Time of Slavery." *South Atlantic Quarterly* 101 (4): 757–777. https://doi.org/10.1215/00382876-101-4-757.

Hawk, Byron. 2018. *Resounding the Rhetorical: Composition as a Quasi-Object*. Pittsburgh, PA: University of Pittsburgh Press.

Hesford, Wendy. 2011. *Spectacular Rhetorics: Human Rights Visions, Recognitions, Feminisms*. Durham, NC: Duke University Press.

Hidalgo, Alexandria. 2021. "'A Response to Cushman, Baca, and García's *College English* Introduction." *Constellations: A Cultural Rhetorics Publishing Space* 4: 2–14.

Hinton, Elizabeth. 2016. *From the War on Poverty to the War on Crime: The Making of Mass Incarceration in America*. Cambridge, MA: Harvard University Press.

Horner, Bruce, Samantha NeCamp, and Christiane Donahue. 2011. "Toward a Multilingual Composition Scholarship: From English Only to a Translingual Norm." *College Composition and Communication* 80 (2): 105–132.

Inoue, Asao B. 2015. *Antiracist Writing Assessment Ecologies: Teaching and Assessing Writing for a Socially Just Future*. Anderson, SC: Parlor Press.

Kelly, Ernece B. 1968. "Murder of the American Dream." *College Composition and Communication* 19 (2): 106–108.

Kennedy, Tammie M., Joyce Irene Middleton, and Krista Ratcliffe. 2005. "The Matter of Whiteness: Or, Why Whiteness Studies Is Important to Rhetoric and Composition Studies." *Rhetoric Review* 24 (4): 359–373.

Kennedy, Tammie M., Joyce Irene Middleton, and Krista Ratcliffe, eds. 2017. Rhetorics of Whiteness: Postracial Hauntings in Popular Culture, Social Media, and Education. Carbondale: SIU Press.

King, Martin Luther, Jr. 1963. "Letter from Birmingham Jail." In *The Norton Anthology of African American Literature*, edited by Henry Louis Gates Jr. and Nellie Y. McKay, 1854–1866. New York: W. W. Norton & Company.

Krug, Jessica. 2020. "The Truth, and the Anti-Black Violence of My Lies." Medium, September 3. www.medium.com/@jessakrug/the-truth-and-the-anti -black-violence-of-my-lies-9a9621401f85.

Kynard, Carmen. 2013. *Vernacular Insurrections: Race, Black Protest, and the New Century in Composition-Literacies Studies*. Albany: State University of New York Press.

Lee, Harper. 1960. *To Kill a Mockingbird*. New York: Grand Central Publishing.

Lowery, Wesley, and Michael Miller. 2015. "Activist Shaun King Says Man on Birth Certificate Isn't His Biological Father." *Washington Post.*, August 20. https:// www.washingtonpost.com/news/post-nation/wp/2015/08/20/activist-shaun -king-says-man-on-birth-certificate-isnt-his-biological-father/.

MacDonald, Katie. 2016. "Calls for Educating Girls in the Third World: Futurity, Girls and the 'Third World Woman.'" *Gender, Place, and Culture: A Journal of Feminist Geography* 23 (1): 1–17.

Macrorie, Ken. 1970. *Uptaught*. Portsmouth, NH: Boynton/Cook Publishers.

Maraj, Louis M. 2020. *Black or Right: Anti/Racist Campus Rhetorics*. Logan: Utah State University Press.

Maraj, Louis M. 2022. "Unlike Conventional Form(s) Of: Beyond Reparative Antiracism." *Composition Studies* 50 (3): 40–58.

Martinez, Aja Y. 2020. *Counterstory: The Rhetoric and Writing of Critical Race Theory*. Urbana, IL: Conference on College Composition and Communication.

McCarthy, Leslie G. 2020. "Annual Day of Dialogue and Action Explores University Commitment to Diversity and Inclusion." Washington Univer-

sity in St. Louis—The Source, February 20. https://source.wustl.edu/2020
/02/annual-day-of-dialogue-action-explores-university-commitment-to
-diversity-and-inclusion/.

McGreal, Chris. 2015. "Rachel Dolezal: 'I Wasn't Identifying as Black to Upset People. I Was Being Me.'" *The Guardian*. December 13. https://www
.theguardian.com/us-news/2015/dec/13/rachel-dolezal-i-wasnt-identifying
-as-black-to-upset-people-i-was-being-me.

McKittrick, Katherine. 2006. *Demonic Grounds: Black Women and the Cartogra-
phies of Struggle*. Minneapolis: University of Minnesota Press.

Melamed, Jodi. 2011. *Represent and Destroy: Rationalizing Violence in the New
Racial Capitalism*. Minneapolis: University of Minnesota Press.

Mills, Charles W. 2007. "White Ignorance." In *Race and Epistemologies of Ignorance*, edited by Shannon Sullivan and Nancy Tuana, 11–38. Albany: State
University of New York Press.

Mills, Charles W. 2014. "WHITE TIME: The Chronic Injustice of Ideal Theory."
Du Bois Review: Social Science Research on Race 11 (1): 27–42. https://doi.org/10
.1017/S1742058X14000022.

Mohanty, Chandra T. 1984. "Under Western Eyes: Feminist Scholarship and
Colonial Discourses." *Boundary 2* 12 (3): 333–358.

Morrison, Toni. 1992. *Playing in the Dark: Whiteness and the Literary Imagination*.
Cambridge, MA: Harvard University Press.

Myrdal, Gunnar. 1944. *An American Dilemma: The Negro Problem and Modern
Democracy*, New York: Harper & Brothers.

Ngo, Helen. 2019. "'Get Over It'? Racialised Temporalities and Bodily Orientations in Time." *Journal of Intercultural Studies* 40 (2): 239–253. https://doi.org
/10.1080/07256868.2019.1577231.

Ohio State University Wexner Medical Center. 2020. "21-Day Anti-Racism
Challenge." Ohio State University Wexner Medical Center. Accessed July 22,
2024. http://wexnermedical.osu.edu/-/media/files/wexnermedical/about-us
/diversity/finalantiracism21daychallenge.pdf.

Parks, Stephen. 2000. *Class Politics: The Movement for the Students' Right to Their
Own Language*. Champaign, IL: National Council of Teachers of English
(NCTE).

Pough, Gwendolyn D. 2004. *Check It While I Wreck It: Black Womanhood, Hip-
Hop Culture, and the Public Sphere*. Boston: Northeastern University Press.

Quijano, Aníbal. 2000. "Coloniality of Power, Eurocentrism, and Latin America." *Nepantla: Views from South* 1 (3): 533–580.

Ratcliffe, Krista. 2005. *Rhetorical Listening: Identification, Gender, Whiteness*.
Carbondale: Southern Illinois University Press.

Reddy, Chandan. 1998. "Home, Houses, Nonidentity: 'Paris Is Burning,'" *Burning Down the House: Recycling Domesticity*, edited by Rosemary Marangoly
George, 355–379. Boulder: Boulder Westview Press.

Rhodes, Jacqueline, and Jonathan Alexander. 2014. "Reimagining the Social Turn: New Work from the Field." *College English* 76 (6): 481–487.

Rickert, Thomas. 2013. *Ambient Rhetoric: The Attunements of Rhetorical Being.* Pittsburgh, PA: University of Pittsburgh Press.

Robinson, Cedric J. 1983. *Black Marxism: The Making of the Black Radical Tradition.* London: Zed Books.

Rockmore, Tom. 1997. *On Heidegger's Nazism and Philosophy.* Berkeley: University of California Press.

Ruiz, Iris D., and Raúl Sánchez. 2016. *Decolonizing Rhetoric and Composition Studies: New Latinx Keywords for Theory and Pedagogy,* London: Palgrave Macmillan/Springer.

Ryden, Wendy, and Ian Marshall. 2013. Reading, Writing, and the Rhetorics of Whiteness. New York: Routledge.

Sano-Franchini, Jennifer Lee, Terese Guinsatao Monberg, and K. Hyoejin Yoon. 2017. *Building a Community, Having a Home: A History of the Conference on College Composition and Communication: Asian/Asian American Caucus.* Anderson, SC: Parlor Press.

Sensoy, Özlem, and Elizabeth Marshall. 2010. "Missionary Girl Power: Saving the 'Third World' One Girl at a Time." *Gender and Education* 22 (3): 295–311.

Smitherman, Geneva. 1977. *Talkin and Testifyin: The Language of Black America.* Boston: Houghton Mifflin.

Smitherman, Geneva. 1995. "'Students' Right to Their Own Language': A Retrospective." *English Journal* 84 (1): 21–27. https://doi.org/10.2307/820470.

Smitherman, Geneva. 2003. "The Historical Struggle for Language Rights in the CCCC." In *Language Diversity in the Classroom: From Intention to Practice,* edited by Victor Villanueva and Geneva Smitherman, 7–39. Carbondale: Southern Illinois University Press.

Trimbur, John. 2019. "Composition's Left and the Struggle for Revolutionary Consciousness." In *Writing Democracy: The Political Turn In and Beyond the Trump Era,* edited by Shannon Carter, Deborah Mutnick, Stephen Parks, and Jessica Pauszek, 27–50. New York: Routledge. https://www.taylorfrancis.com/chapters/composition-left-struggle-revolutionary-consciousness-john-trimbur/e/10.4324/9780429469169-2.

Twain, Mark. 1884. *The Adventures of Huckleberry Finn.* London: Chatto & Windus / Charles L. Webster and Company.

"2019 #Communicationsowhite Controversy." 2019. #Communicationsowhite Controversy. http://2019commsowhitecontroversy.simplesite.com/.

Washington, Myra. 2020. "Woke Skin, White Masks: Race and Communication Studies." *Communication and Critical/Cultural Studies* 17 (2): 261–266.

Williams, Patricia J. 1991. *The Alchemy of Race and Rights.* Boston: Harvard University Press.

Wolin, Richard. 2023. *Heidegger in Ruins: Between Philosophy and Ideology*. New Haven, CT: Yale University Press.

Wright, Michelle M. 2015. Physics of Blackness: Beyond the Middle Passage Epistemology. Minneapolis: University of Minnesota Press.

Yancey, Kathleen Blake. 2018. "Mapping the Turn to Disciplinarity: A Historical Analysis of Composition's Trajectory and Its Current Moment." In *Composition, Rhetoric, and Disciplinarity*, 15–35. Denver, CO: Utah State University Press.

Yancy, George. 2017. *Black Bodies, White Gazes: The Continuing Significance of Race in America*. Lanham, MD: Rowman & Littlefield.

Ziyad, Hari. 2020. "The Stories and Lies of Jess Krug." *Vanity Fair*, December 17. https://www.vanityfair.com/style/2020/12/the-stories-and-lies-of-jess-krug.

2 · Violent (Re)construction(s)

Gaslighting "Abolition" in US Educational History

Contemporary understandings (or the shaping thereof) of historical events have become one of several ideological battlegrounds in the US at a time when, globally, ultraconservative political representation has gained much traction. As this phenomenon relates specifically to the academy, "critical race theory," for instance, has emerged since 2020 as a catch-all straw man used to argue against the teaching/facing of historical trauma in American classrooms. Though the school of thought emerged in legal studies over thirty years ago, its scapegoating by those with far-right beliefs in the US as almost metonymic signification for "all that is not white" in education or intellectualism (arguably) reorients how academics temporally engage the well-trodden theoretical framework.[1] Consequently, the second Trump presidential administration has sought to eradicate wholesale any race-conscious educational policy, infrastructure, or resource posthaste. On the flipside, (relatively) not very long ago Columbus Day was commemorated in the US with parades and public displays of Italian-American pride

---

1 See Martinez (2020) and, particularly, its afterlives in writing studies scholarship.

https://doi.org/10.7330/9781646428489.c002

and country band "The Chicks" were "The Dixie Chicks"—who, after declaring their shame that US President George W. Bush shared their Texan roots in 2003, were blacklisted in their musical genre. As testament to major shifts in how history might be signified and received publicly, according to *The Washington Post*, 155 Confederate memorials and monuments were removed from US public spaces between 2015 and 2020; only five had been removed between 1865 and 2014 (Berkowitz and Blanco 2020). These examples illustrate not simply the tense role that perceptions of violent histories play in relation to identity (racial, national, and otherwise) along with how those perceptions can change over time but also the importance of terminology, signification, and context mobilized in relation to those histories. To look closely at far-right rhetoric for a moment or two, consider the following summer 2023 political events in the US and the UK.

On July 19 that year the Florida Department of Education unveiled new standards for the teaching of US history in the state's middle schools. Two days later Florida Governor Ron DeSantis, then a Republican Party presidential candidate, defended these changes, which "include teaching 'how slaves developed skills which, in some instances, could be applied for their personal benefit.'" Vice President Kamala Harris, among several others, spoke out against these standards as "propaganda" and suddenly "Black history" and the teaching of it arose as a hot topic for political debate well outside of February (Olorunnipa et al. 2023). While on par with DeSantis's "anti-woke" agenda, this particular educational mandate notably attempts not just to erase slavery's violence but instead frames the kidnap, human trafficking, and enslavement of Black peoples as for their social net gain, a pedagogical benefit, and, significantly, a kind of benevolence granted on the part of slavers. Worth noting, the "personal benefit" angle converges at the intersection of neoliberal bootstrap thinking and racialized tropes of Black people as "lazy," with the qualifier "could" suggesting that those "slaves" who did not apply their captivity and torture to their individual advantage missed out on their opportunity for social uplift. The "silver lining" narrative promoted in the Florida Department of Education's revision of history functions as a benevolent gaslight by rescripting egregious anti-Black violence as a gift.

Across the pond only a month later, Nick Buckley MBE (Member of the Order of the British Empire)—British "charity" worker and independent political candidate in the 2024 race for mayor of Great Manchester—tweeted a graphic with a message that closely aligns with the new middle school standards for teaching US history in Florida. Backgrounded by the Union Jack with Buckley posted to its right, in white all capitalized text, the image reads: "GREAT BRITAIN ENDED THE INTERNATIONAL SLAVE TRADE. NO ONE ELSE DID IT. WE DID IT. SOME GRATITUDE IS OVERDUE" (Buckley 2023). While ignoring the British Empire's contributions as one of the most significant (if not *the* most significant) player in transatlantic slavery, the message rescripts the nation as responsible for the trade's demise. In Buckley's vision, then, Great Britain ought to be recognized for a major historical antiracist act, with the entire population of the (then? now?) nation a "we"—that first-person plural pronoun, of course, speaking for an unraced collective consciousness. In this example—much like DeSantis's and the Florida Department of Education's—a singular, collectively shared vision of the past does not simply rehabilitate a shameful history of violent anti-Black extraction; it forwards, rather, an alternate past in which those responsible for that extraction champion the plights of enslaved and freed Black peoples. Buckley's graphic, perhaps, goes one step further than the previous example to suggest ingratitude (by, one can only guess, Black people?) in a boldfaced request for appreciation.

Though these ideologically "conservative" examples spotlight how historical record might be refashioned for contemporary political means, what might audiences miss by categorizing the pattern noted in the above rhetoric as a *current* "far-right" phenomenon? More directly, if we place pressure on Buckley's message informed by material histories of abolition and focused on the players who, in its time and immediate (and not so immediate) aftermath, largely took public responsibility for the event of transatlantic slavery's ending, might an insidious rhetorical similarity emerge? Taking the Florida Department of Education's and

Buckley's points of entry together to excavate how publicly vocal "abolitionists" frame "abolitionist pedagogy" (in today's terms) in the time of US slavery's abolition—manifested in published educational material for newly freed Black people in this case—could help illumine the long arc of the benevolent gaslight as a function of Western racialization. Prior to that departure, however, zooming in on just how the communicative signifier "abolition" gets taken up within rhetoric and writing studies as intellectual fields might offer some important context for an exploration of "abolitionist pedagogy" situated closely to (perhaps) its most important connotative historical precedent.

In "Terms" of Abolition

"Abolition"—the act of abandoning a system or practice—as a term carries (and has carried) varied kinds of symbolic weight in rhetoric and writing studies and beyond. In maybe its most temporally pressing senses, it evokes alliance with phrases like "abolish the police"—particularly relevant in the aftermath of summer 2020's racial violence in the US—and teaching-in-prisons programs, and it finds currency in anti-carceral connotations and metaphors. Indeed, outside the academy, the marker perhaps most widely refers to prison abolition movements—such as #8toabolition, which specifically emerged in 2020. In the field, one could look to a 2023 call-for-papers for a special issue of the nascent journal *Rhetoric, Politics & Culture*, edited by Logan Rae Gomez, Matthew Houdek, and Robert Mejia, on "Rhetoric and the Abolitionist Horizon," for context. The call orients its understanding of "abolitionist rhetoric" by naming various activist collectives as "abolitionist groups," while grounding dimensions of it in the theories of Black women activists like Mariame Kaba and Ruth Wilson Gilmore (Rhetoric, Politics, and Culture 2023). Meanwhile, earlier that year the Conference on College Composition and Communication (CCCC) featured rhetoric/writing scholar and poet Stacey Waite and poet/activist Andrea Ab-Karam's (2023) keynote address, "'about to happen'/'poetry as forces': abolitionist poetics," spotlighting rhetoric and writing's deepened investments in this recent conceptualization of social justice–oriented work. Alongside these developments, the likes of Bettina Love lead and sustain parallel debates in related fields, such as educational theory, while even in disciplines as far afield as criminology, scholars such as Vicki Chartrand and Justin Piché (2019) engage the notion. In Love's landmark *We Want to Do More Than Survive: Abolitionist Teaching and the Pursuit of Educational Freedom*, for instance, "abolitionist teaching" refers to "the practice of working in solidarity with communities of color while drawing on the imagination, creativity, refusal, (re)membering, visionary thinking, healing, rebellious spirit, boldness, determination, and subversiveness of abolitionists to eradicate injustice in and outside of schools" (2019, 2). Love highlights figures like Ella Baker, Bayard Rustin, Angela Davis, and Fannie Lou Hamer to exemplify those from whom one may learn of pedagogies beyond mere institutional reform (2019, 2). But just what does "abolitionist" as a descriptor for social justice–oriented politics signify? What particular systems or practices does rhetoric and writing intend to abandon so it might free itself of "carceral logics" when the field—exemplified by its practitioners and scholars—still obviously operates within oppressive matrixes borne out in racial capitalism? And does the framework simply offer more reform (at the level of particular modes of thinking or action) or true disavowal (manifested in genuine abandonment of the project of the university altogether)?

Along a similar dismantle-or-reform dialectic, "abolition" in writing studies criticism proper once invoked (and maybe still invokes?) debates around whether first-year writing ought to continue to exist. In the 1990s through the early aughts, "the new abolitionists," led by figures such as Robert J. Connors (1995), took cues from Sharon Crowley's (1991) "A Personal Essay on Freshman English," which suggests making the course at the crux of composition studies an elective as the means by which to challenge "the course's historical function as a repressive instrument of student (and teacher) legitimation" (170). And while Maureen Daly Goggin and Susan Kay Miller (2000) confront the binary terms of the debate (revolution versus reformation) and even the racially problematic referentiality of "abolitionist" (104n3), the discursive historical context of "abolition" still remains part of the field's history, as Connors (1995) delineates, dating back to the 1890s. But what of teaching's relationships to those who, in North American contexts, first labeled themselves "abolitionists"—white nineteenth-century figures who "championed" the literal emancipation of enslaved Africans? Or, relatedly, what of the orientations of those who, at the time of the abolition of slavery in the US, took on public, pedagogical roles?

In unpacking the (co-)operations of anti-Black (anti)racism and educational praxis, this chapter rummages the post-emancipation US pedagogical texts of three such figures: Clinton Bowen Fisk, Rev. Jared Bell Waterbury, and Lydia Maria Child. Their texts—Fisk's (1866) *Plain Counsels for Freedmen: In Sixteen Brief Lectures*; Waterbury's (1864) *Friendly Counsels for Freedmen*; and Child's (1865) *The Freedmen's Book*—provide a historical snapshot of the ways in which those who framed themselves "abolitionists" in the time of transatlantic slavery offered their formerly enslaved audience a kind of prototypical benevolent gaslight by reconstructing the violent realities of chattel slavery as a teaching moment from which this audience (and consequently larger society) could benefit—while projecting themselves and their historical afterlives "antiracist." The succeeding sections (1) situate this chapter's arguments in longstanding epistemological trajectories and other relevant Black studies and anticolonial scholarship; (2) offer biographical/contextual sketches of Fisk, Waterbury, and Child while previewing the material histories of their published educational material in focus; and (3) posit close readings of the texts in question. The third segment specifically highlights how the characterization of the industry of slavery, an emphasis on the "individual responsibility" of the formerly enslaved, and the rhetorical structure of Reconstruction pedagogical texts contribute to the regurgitation of benevolent gaslighting as an integral discursive facet of early US educational history. These particular workings of this technology of whiteness manifest at the interrelated levels of each individual abolitionist's posturing, in the rhetorical force of freedmen's primers as a genre of educational material in their zeitgeist, and as a broader perspective on the nature of (white and whitened) abolitionism. From such a perspective, in these abolitionists' flight to the "teaching moment" of Reconstruction, they rescript the institution of chattel slavery as that which inaugurates the linear social "progress" of all now called "free" or "man" or "freedman" (consequently placing themselves on the "right" side of history).

Fisk's (1866), Waterbury's (1864), and Child's (1865) primers represent just a few specifically genre-d "pedagogical" examples of the kind of broader philosophical approach that Buckley speaks on behalf of in his August 2023 tweet. In Buckley's line of thinking, responsibility—in the local politician's mind, national responsibility—for the violences of transatlantic slavery disappears because members of the same group supposedly brought about its ending. This logic aligns with the tautological notion that the US as a national entity has "progressed" on race relations because of the event of the Civil Rights Act of 1964—where a change in law marks a linear path to morality in which a nation "learns" from the violences of the past—and bears out in extremity in the Florida Department of Education's revisionist history that slavery *helped* the enslaved. As a challenge to the popular mobilization of such thinking in the face of blatant anti-Blackness and forms of non-Black racisms, this chapter destabilizes the neat narratives that these logics promote, at both the levels of wider social consciousness and, specifically, at local tiers of educational history as they relate to the question of "abolitionism." Ultimately, it suggests that illuming how whiteness mobilized "abolitionism" for its racializing purposes in the past may perhaps reveal the extent of the framework's rhetorical weight in contemporary usage.

Epistemological Lineages

The project to shatter the illusion that abolition of the transatlantic slave trade sprang mainly from moral or humanitarian impulses stretches back to the groundbreaking work of historian, politician, and first prime minister of Trinidad and Tobago, Eric Eustace Williams. Via an economic history argument, Williams's 1944 *Capitalism and Slavery* illustrates not only how the trade financed the British Industrial Revolution but also, importantly, how the early nineteenth-century decline in British slavery's profitability in the Caribbean led to abolition as a prudent economic solution to diminishing returns. The monograph takes specific aim at how British historians frame and had framed the event of abolition instead as an humanitarian act (Williams 1944), "challenging the traditional view that the colonies were more the recipients of metropolitan benevolence and less the principal agents in the imperial power's prosperity" (Palmer 1994, xxi). It, therefore, underscores how dominant ways of knowing history—in its time and for thirteen decades prior—mobilized the violence of slavery (obscured in a focus on its end) as fuel for an imperial narrative of antiracist sentimentality on behalf of the British people. In the monograph's conclusion, Williams (1944) lucidly declares:

> Politics and morals in the abstract make no sense. We find the British statesmen and publicists defending slavery today, abusing slavery tomorrow, defending slavery the day after. Today they are imperialist, the next day anti-imperialist, and equally pro-imperialist a generation after. And always with the same vehemence. The defence or attack is always on the high moral or political plane . . . historians, writing a hundred years after, have no excuse for continuing to wrap the real interests in confusion. Even the great mass movements, and the anti-slavery mass movement was one of the greatest of these, show a curious affinity with the rise and development of new interests and the necessity of the destruction of the old. (211)

Boldly questioning the manipulation of historical memory as impetus for moral high ground, *Capitalism and Slavery* epistemically disarrays prevailing historical thought, coming close to describing the benevolent gaslight in full.

At the time of its publication, British culture and its major historians had for over a century worked hand in hand to forward the idea that it had been humanitarianism (led by the likes of William Wilberforce) that spurred the passage of the Slavery Abolition Act of 1833. As Matthew Wyman-McCarthy (2018, 2–3) outlines, this epistemological trajectory spans histories of abolitionism published from as early as 1808 (only a year after the British colonial trade was outlawed) by Thomas Clarkson, to assertions by Wilberforce's sons that abolition reflected "the moral feelings of a nation" (Wilberforce 1838, 183), to Oxford historian Reginald Coupland ([1933] 1964)—at whom Williams took direct aim—who described at the centennial of the Abolition Act a post–American Revolutionary War "new philanthropy" in British politics (see also Klingberg 1926, Lecky 1869, Seely 1883, Stock 1899). The field of colonial British history did not very much appreciate Williams's argument, as it sought to undermine the zeitgeist's prevalent historiographical stance, which embraced the tenet that imperial legislative changes equated to historical advancement—think, maybe again, here of the previous section's example of the US Civil Rights Act.

Capitalism and Slavery, moreover, ruptured the field of colonial history (and possibly history in toto), prompting much criticism since its publication. These challenges include questions about the study's economic data and its analysis (therefore clouding the issue of British reliance on slavery's profits for industrial progress) as well as more pointed confrontation with the question of moralism's involvement in abolition.[2] Seymour Drescher (1987), notably, asserts that moral fervor from the British electorate directly resulted in the 1807 abolition of the trade. Regardless of these critiques, Drescher (1987) himself—among others who praised the work including Kenneth Morgan (2004) and Selwyn Carrington (1984)—names the monograph a "classic" for "reorient[ing] our most basic way of viewing . . . a concept"

---

2 For criticisms mainly of how Williams presents the quantifiable share of the British economy for which slavery's profits accounted, see Engerman (1972), Heuman (1999), Richardson (1998), and Ward (1998).

(180). Prolific Barbadian historian Sir Hilary Beckles (1984) notes the "invaluable importance" of it as "sound intellectual ammunition" for "the anti-imperialist/anti-colonial thrust" of the Black Nationalist movement in the Caribbean (172). *Capitalism and Slavery*, therefore, pronouncedly disrupts the means by which historians and activists would (come to) know history, ushering in angles into dismissing forms of mis-signified, insidious, and packaged-as-gracious white supremacist knowledge/culture projects.

On the US front, Black feminist theorist and historian Saidiya Hartman's (1997) *Scenes of Subjection: Terror, Slavery, and Self-Making in Nineteenth-Century America* marks an important point of departure for thinking through how slavery's subjugating mechanisms—and significantly the quotidian features of its violences—extend across the eventline of emancipation. Hartman's reading of various "scenes" (from material like diaries, slave narratives, legal cases, theatre, etc.) prompts an understanding of how "individual will" and "responsibility" operate across pre-emancipation and Reconstruction contexts, "concerned with the savage encroachments of power that take place through notions of reform, consent, and protection" (5)—the latter especially important in how the "benevolence" of the US Reconstruction period exemplifies and prefigures gaslighting pedagogies to come.

Scenes of Subjection's (Hartman 1997) claims about enslavement's mechanisms's continuation through illusions of legislative "freedom" from bondage, together with the book's assertions about their impacts on Black subject formation in what Hartman later terms "the afterlives of slavery" (2007, 6), offer with them a radical break in views of American history and historiography as well as in theorizing Blackness. Important to Hartman's later path-paving, creatively inflected work in *Lose Your Mother* (2007) and *Wayward Lives, Beautiful Experiments: Intimate Histories of Riotous Black Girls, Troublesome Women, and Queer Radicals* (2019), *Scenes of Subjection*'s propositions would also prove crucial to the coalescing of Afropessimist philosophy: Its fundamental stance that "Blackness is coterminous with Slaveness" (Wilderson 2015, n.p.) emanates from a reading of Hartman's arguments.[3] Hartman's (1997) book also sketches the critical landscape against which Christina Sharpe's ground-breaking *In the Wake: On Blackness and Being* (2016)—which tenders a complex analysis of the ways in which Black diasporic lives remain temporally animated in slavery's afterlives—could be set. One might, therefore, situate the operations of the benevolent gaslight highlighted within this chapter against more historically contemporary examples (shared elsewhere in *The Benevolent Gaslight*) in the scope of Sharpe's Hartman-informed theory. Moreover, Hartman's *Scenes*—in interrogating how to know "freedom" in relation to the sustained project of white supremacist domination, the *longue durée* of transatlantic slavery—reveals yet another epistemological fracture in grappling with history and historiography. Like Williams's (1944) *Capitalism and Slavery*, *Scenes* (Hartman 1997) thus viscerally textures this chapter's foray into links between abolitionism (and its pedagogies) and the benevolent gaslight as a technology of racialization.

More granularly, Hartman's (1997) monograph emphasizes how "it was often the case that benevolent correctives and declarations of slave humanity intensified the brutal exercise of power upon the captive body rather than ameliorating the chattel condition" (5). In light of the former, *Scenes* takes to task the freedmen's primers that occupy the attention of this chapter's close readings. Along with her concurrent analysis of Fisk's (1866) and Waterbury's (1864) texts, Hartman reads Isaac Brinckerhoff's (1864) *Advice to Freedmen* and Helen E. Brown's (1864) *John Freeman and His Family*, a work of fiction. "Textbooks" like these four, Hartman (1997) contends, "aimed to instill rational ideals of material acquisition and social restraint and correct 'absolute' notions of freedom and the excesses and indulgences that resulted from entertaining such 'farflung' conceptions" (129). While *Scenes* focuses on the

---

3 Wilderson (2020, 13) spotlights this correlation in highlighting the following passage from Hartman: "The slave is neither civic man nor free worker but excluded from the narrative of 'we the people' that effects the linkage of the modern individual and the state . . . The everyday practices of the enslaved occur in the default of the political, in the absence of the rights of man or the assurances of the self-possessed individual, and perhaps even without a 'person,' in the usual meaning of the term" (Hartman 1997, 65). See also Hartman and Wilderson (2003).

contradiction of freedom and their relation to Black subject formation (Hartman 1997), this chapter builds on the foundations of that analysis in gauging how these primers' rhetoric engages the white "gift" of freedom in concert with slavery's attendant (and in Hartman's conception post-"emancipation") violences.

Adjacent to Williams's (1944) and Hartman's (1997) approach to historical knowledge and its making, two further studies suggest pertinence—though somewhat secondary in comparison—to the proceeding sections. Erin Austin Dwyer's (2021) book-length study of affect in US slavery, *Mastering Emotions*, avers that emotions functioned as a critical discourse in white/Black relations during the era for slaveholders, the enslaved, and free(d) Black people, with each group mobilizing them for their particular sociopolitical purposes. Meanwhile, the framework of "imperial benevolence" grounds the studies in the edited collection *Burden or Benefit?* (2008) (edited by Helen Gilbert and Chris Tiffin), with the concept describing a function of "benevolent empire: a conception of control that acts not for itself but for the controlled" (6). The collection's essays range from the framework's stakes in the colonial world of the 1800s to the postcolonial twenty-first century where foreign aid and Western feminists become subjects of critique. Departing, however, from what Gilbert and Tiffin (2008) return to as a "paradox" in the collection's introduction (6), this chapter apprehends the benevolent gaslight in US Reconstruction contexts as far more sinister than elastic.

Objects of Study

What renowned African American history scholar Carter Godwin Woodson would come to describe as the (titular) *Mis-Education of the Negro* in 1933—how US education to that point afforded Black people a process of indoctrination into white cultural values that perpetuated that culture's sustained superiority—plays out vividly in the works of the three authors under scrutiny. Dominant versions of US history and US public sentiment (and even work in rhetoric and writing studies proper, in one instance), however, still remember these figures (particularly Fisk and Child) fondly.

Immortalized while still alive in a published biography by Alphonso Alva Hopkins (1888), Clayton Bowen Fisk (1828–1890) ran for US president in 1888 as the Prohibition Party's candidate and served as a senior officer in the Bureau of Refugees, Freedmen and Abandoned Lands (known as the Freedmen's Bureau)—a government entity in early US Reconstruction officially responsible for the welfare of formerly enslaved Black people. Fisk also served in the Union Army from 1861. Hopkins (1888) often deploys the term "abolitionist" to describe Fisk with forceful adjectival/contextual markers, such as "Abolitionist as from boyhood" (51); his "early political predilections were all of the old-fashioned abolitionist sort" (169); "he believed intensely in the abolition of slavery" (53); and in voting he made "abolition sentiments the final test of a nominee" (169). These beliefs, accordingly, had developed from time spent with his stepfather, William Smith, and his compatriot Deacon Wright, both of whom Hopkins identifies as abolitionists. Fisk built fires for their meetings, "breathed now an intenser radical atmosphere than ever" as "the Smith homestead was a section of the Underground Railroad, and, boy as he was, Clinton became a sub-conductor of that famous thoroughfare" (Hopkins 1888, 32). Deeply entrenched in the abolitionist mission, Hopkins's biography proves less important now to history than Fisk's $30,000 endowment of Fisk University (originally known as Fisk Free Colored School), a private historically Black liberal arts college in Nashville, Tennessee (Warner 1964, 155).

Fewer descriptors of Rev. Jared Bell Waterbury DD's (1799–1876) life and times survive to the present day. Waterbury, a Yale, Princeton Seminary, and Union College graduate and Presbyterian minister, however, published sermons, tracts, creative works, and "over thirty" larger volumes during his seventy-seven years (Yale University 1877, 248). These include *Advice to a Young Christian*, (1830), *Considerations for Young Men* (1832); *The Happy Christian: or, Piety the Only Foundation of True and Substantial Joy* (1838); and *Southern Planters and Freedmen*

(1863), among others. One nineteenth-century biblical encyclopedia describes *Advice to a Young Christian* as "widely read and very useful" (M'Clintock and Strong, 886). Waterbury also regularly "wrote much for the religious press" (887). As "a preacher of unusual excellence and power," he served throughout New England, in his home city New York; in Hatfield, Massachusetts; New Hampshire; Boston; Connecticut; and, during the Civil War, as secretary for the Christian Commission's Brooklyn and Long Island branch, supplying literature and ministry to the Union Army (M'Clintock and Strong 1877, 887; Yale University 1877, 248). Unlike Fisk and, most pronouncedly, Child, historical record does not name Waterbury via the signifier "abolitionist," though his published material in the 1860s employs evangelical abolitionist sentiment to frame the event of emancipation. *Southern Planters and Freedmen* (along with *Friendly Counsels* [1864]), for instance, attributes the end of slavery to the "providence of God" (Waterbury 1863, 5). Nevertheless, published histories remember Waterbury as "faithful, sympathetic, and earnest" (M'Clintock and Strong 1877, 887).

Of the three figures studied in this chapter, the memorialization of Lydia Maria Child (1802–1880) as "antiracist" (in contemporary parlance) perhaps looms largest. In 2007 both the National Women's Hall of Fame and the National Abolition Hall of Fame inducted Child into their honor rolls. In the past three decades, literary critic Carolyn L. Karcher's (1994) 800-page *The First Woman of the Republic*, historican Lori J. Kenschaft's (2002) "Oxford Portrait," and philosopher Lydia Moland's 2022 biography exemplify the recent scholarly attention directed at Child's life and oeuvre—the latter spanning most every genre of writing popular in the nineteenth century: from journalism, to fiction, to advice book, to children's literature, to historical novel, and more. Her *Frugal Housewife* (1829)—which shared recipes and everyday "wisdom"—according to Thomas Wentworth Higginson in 1899—"proved so popular that in 1836 it had reached its twentieth edition, and in 1855, its thirty-third" (117). When it took political aim, Child's published body of work targeted women's rights, Indigenous rights, and—most markedly—slavery's abolition. Her convictions to abolitionism most clearly first emerged from 1930 onward in the pages of *Juvenile Miscellany* (Karcher 1994, 158)—a then-ongoing children's periodical—but Child's 1833 *An Appeal in Favor of That Class of Americans Called Africans* stirred the proverbial literati and cultural pot on its release. Kenshaft (2002) notes "future senator and congressional leader of the abolitionist cause," Charles Sumner, and abolitionist orator Wendell Phillips as just two who openly credit the book with "awakening [them] to the injustice of slavery" (6). Likewise, Karcher (1994) contends that in *Appeal* Child offers the abolitionist movement its first comprehensive analysis of US slavery with a scope so exhaustive no other writer after her would attempt its range (183). Rhetorical studies scholar Jessica Enoch (2008) adds that the book marked Child's "new role as antislavery educator" (49)—a role that would continue decades on in *The Freedmen's Book* (1865).

Following the Civil War, the end of slavery in the US witnessed a veritable flood of published educational material directed at the formerly enslaved. Historian Ronald E. Butchart (2016) emphasizes the publication speed of this material as an understudied aspect of Reconstruction history, explaining:

> Organizations and writers interested in the freed slaves created, in remarkably short time, primers, spellers, readers, and other didactic texts for the freedmen's schools and for [B]lack adult education classes. The earliest were published by 1863, a mere 2 years after the outbreak of war; by 1866, over a dozen primers, readers, monthly papers, and other text material for [S]outhern [B]lack schools had appeared. (75)

One such organization, the American Tract Society—a nonprofit, evangelical organization founded in 1825—published both Fisk's (1866) *Plain Counsels* and Waterbury's (1864) *Friendly Counsels*, among a plethora of other such texts. The society even founded a Black school in Washington, DC, to "test the market" for its materials. Child's (1865) *The Freedmen's Book*, however, represents one of two outliers in the flurry of post-emancipation pedagogical manuals. She published it independently, and it took a distinct shape—and, at 277 pages, proved the lengthiest in the genre—in contrast to other such materials of its time (Butchart 2016, 75). In terms of content, Fisk's (1866) and Waterbury's (1864) texts also closely align with the "advice book" genre, while Child's offers much more of an anthology of writings with varied genre conventions. The pages of *The Freedmen's Record* sing praises of Child's book, marking it "fully appreciated and enjoyed by those for whom it was written," with one schoolteacher claiming it sparks "a wonderful amount of good among these people" ("The Freedmen's Book" 1866, 69). "Good," of course, in these senses, communicates the affective and cultural interests of white teachers and white society writ large at the time. As another entry in *The Freedmen's Record* four years later explains—while citing the effect of Child's and other pedagogical texts on both children and adult learners—"they seem to appreciate the true value of [education]," predicting that "after the seed of virtue and knowledge, and the minds of the people have become educated, the rank weed of *vice*, which is casting its baneful influence on society, will soon wither and die." This schoolteacher promises to "proceed cheerfully" henceforth with this benevolent mission (Wilson 1870, 62). As Hartman (1997) convincingly asserts, as plantation ceremony "endeavored to make discipline a pleasure and vice versa" (43), these kinds of pedagogical texts stretch that pleasurable disciplining across the demarcating line of emancipation's event, "exposed by the centrality of prohibition and punishment, which were relied upon in the fashioning of liberal individualism" (129). The narrativizing of slavery (and its end) across Fisk's (1866), Waterbury's (1864), and Child's (1865) educational materials arguably operates in service of this kind of disciplining, whereby slavery's violence becomes a tool for emotional manipulation—one graciously given to forward the "antiracist" work of Reconstruction educators (whether intentional or not).

(Re)constructing Slavery and Abolition

Much in the vein of the 2023 changes to education standards in Floridian teaching of history, the narrative (re)construction of US chattel slavery as something beyond an excessively violent and extractive industry permeates Reconstruction pedagogical texts. This kind of rescripting of racial trauma lies at the heart of the benevolent gaslight as technology for making racial domination. While not as extreme as to present purely "net good" readings of slavery, Fisk's (1866) and Waterbury's (1864) primers attempt to place their Black audience in "objective" position relative to their own still quite socially downtrodden conditions of post-emancipation. Of course, such "objectivity" serves as a quintessential epistemological and hermeneutical white stance. As Denise Ferreira da Silva (2007) attests, the bedrock of Western philosophical and anthropological thought formulates a "transparent I": "the subject of transparency, for whom internal reason is an interior guide" where "others of Europe"—those outside of its classification—operate as "subjects of affectability, for whom universal reason remains an exterior ruler" (40). Such a relationship between white author and Black audience palpably marks all three pedagogical texts, but particularly Fisk's (1866) and Waterbury's (1864). Fisk (1866), for instance, urges the freed to live amicably with former masters, emphasizing the bitter resentment that must emerge from losing one's property, investment, and wealth, along with the loss of lives and disablement through the violence of the war. "He has had a hard time of it," Fisk narrates early in his book: "Now it is natural that he should feel sore; that he should grieve over his loss; that he should be slow to adapt himself to the new state of things; and that he should be some years in putting off the airs and manners of a master, just as you find it hard to shake off the habits of slaves" (10–11). In "humanizing" these former masters, Fisk prioritizes their interiorities as the basis for characterizing as "natural . . . that he should feel severe toward you" (11). The equations that *Plain Counsels* unwraps set out from the assertion that whether a slaveowner was "a very good master" or "not so good," "that is all past now" (10)—the rhetoric of "good" deployed in sole relation to itself where an audience may not imagine its flip side or even its graphic underbelly in, say, "vengeful," "wicked," or "quick-tempered." This start-from-scratch argument, therefore, erases the traumas of the past still actualizing in the present while remaining predicated on descriptions of former slaveholders only conjured from a starting point of white "good" and, well, injury (emotional, financial, and/or otherwise). The gaslight, in this instance, finds force in not just foregrounding benevolence but in prompting it as the exclusive available metric from which to gauge the past in endeavors toward the racial "progress" spurred in educating Black people.

Waterbury's (1864) text launches from even less about slavery's conditions, instead crediting "the Almighty's" use of the war as providential and the reason for emancipation. He urges his Black audience to always remain grateful for this gift (3). But he marks freedom, in comparison to enslavement, as "in some respects much better, and in others somewhat worse" (3–4). The rationale for this portrayal embarks from the logic that "Your master, if he was kind, took good care of you" (4) with alternate possibilities—perhaps laden with memories of torture, natal alienation, sexual assault and exploitation, murder, and so forth—absent. Like Fisk's (1866), Waterbury's (1864) book looks backward historically from the perspective of "universal reason" (mobilized in effort to rule his affectable subjects) rather than from any posture of accountability. Its sections on "Honesty," "Lying," and "Purity" claim that the rampant habits of stealing, lying, and sexual promiscuity respectively emerge from, or act as constituent of, enslavement (and therefore related only to Black racialization). But still, these descriptions disappear the force of bondage and those responsible for it. Waterbury, for instance, details lying as "universally practiced among the slaves" (1864, 12); when describing adultery, he declares, "In slavery, this vice or wickedness has not been thought so very bad; and perhaps, in some instances, it may even have been encouraged" (14). In the latter, Waterbury's particular grammatical choice of no subject for who held the privilege to think a vice "bad" and the passive voice of "it may have even been" prove telling. They say nothing of distinct (accountable) actors or, moreover, of *partus sequitur ventrem*, the legal doctrine passed in 1662 Virginia dictating that a child born to an enslaved woman inherits their mother's enslaved position, which encouraged planters to literally increase their wealth through sexual assault and coercion. Moreover, Waterbury's rhetorical maneuvers align with elisions in Western gender theory that cultural theorist Hortense Spillers (1987) highlights in explaining how "the African female subject, under these historic conditions, is not only the target of rape—in one sense, an interiorized violation of body and mind—but also the topic of specifically *externalized* acts of torture and prostration that we imagine as the peculiar province of *male* brutality and torture inflicted by other males" (68). For Waterbury (1864), "adultery" simply amounts to one of many slavish traits of which his audience of freed Black people must rid themselves in pursuit of freedom's ideals. Its violences and those inherently responsible for them vanish in a moral high ground envisioning a new America.

Fisk's (1866) *Plain Counsels* differs only slightly in that it pointedly addresses Black women on the topic of sexuality in Lecture VI. The lecture first conditionally advises: "If in your slave life you have been careless of your morals, now that you are free, live as becomes a free Christian woman" (26). Yet a later lecture, "To Married Folks," more firmly establishes that "when you were slaves you 'took up' with each other and were not taught what a bad thing it was to break God's law of marriage" (31). Much like the driving logic throughout Waterbury's (1864) primer, Fisk's (1866) directives position Black people as willing participants in so-called "vices" without very much important context explaining how slaveholders (and the slave trade proper) benefited from the scenario described in addition to their forcing, and their own forceful, violations of "God's law of marriage" (31). As Hartman (1997, 11) underlines in her read of seduction and sexuality in the period through Harriet Jacobs's writings, "consent is meaningless if refusal is not an option" where "seduction"—assumed in both Fisk's (1866) and

Waterbury's (1864) condemnations—"inevitably entails a calculated misreading or misrecognition of the state of domination." (Hartman 1997, 111). Fisk (1866) nevertheless propels onward in declaring, "But now you can only be sorry for the past" (31), because from his *abolitionist* perspective his Black audience hold responsibility for their alleged "sins." This moral superiority continues in Fisk's lecture on "dishonesty," which, although "not defined to one class, or color, or party" (52), specifically arises out of three "causes," which curiously all happen to befall the formerly enslaved. The first, slavery, "fosters lying and stealing," while the second and third, "poverty" and "idleness," speak to distinct conditions that loom immediately applicable to his audience (52–53). Significantly, Fisk decontextualizes slavery as a cause for dishonesty, reasoning *universally* that "in all countries and in all ages these vices have prevailed among slaves." After the generalization, Fisk makes the point pertinent to claim that with slavery "forever abolished" in the US, "the cause has been removed, although the effects have not ceased" (53). *Plain Counsels* gaslights its audience by relying on these kinds of rhetorical sleights of hand whereby the cultural implications of slavery make an enslaved population morally corrupt—those conditions in some cases made both covertly and overtly the fault of this audience—but those creating those conditions slide by unmentioned. As rhetor, Fisk situates himself as part of the "solution," which entails breaking the dissolute habits that undergird such depravity in the name of American (racial) progress.

All while not detailing any specific violences that slavery may have wrought on Black readers, Fisk urges Black people under these circumstances, however, to "think kindly of your old master" (11). Waterbury (1864), in kind, offers that the "government aided by good people, is ready to lend you a helping hand" (6)—with authors of pedagogical material such as his and Fisk's inherently apprehended among those "good." Indeed, Waterbury believes possessions, property ownership, and investment in family life will eventually fashion Black people worthy of a kind of humanity (27), in concert with the affective combination of white benevolence and the now freed Blacks graciously eating

   VIOLENT (RE)CONSTRUCTION(S)

the abuse hurled toward them (as "good" Christians want). On the former front, Fisk (1866) deploys comparable reasoning in the absence of culpable grammatical subjects to explain that "heretofore you had no opportunity to provide homes for yourselves and your families. You were liable to be removed at any time, and it was impossible for you to keep your families together" (60). For all of the traumas of kidnap, isolation, and dispossession, Fisk produces no responsible actor: "You" simply faced the life of objecthood in a forgettable past. And while *Friendly Counsels* lays Waterbury's (1864) kindly posture bare from the jump, *Plain Counsels*—which even in name appeals to a kind of unfettered, objective transparency—frames former masters as primarily "kind" and "honest" (Fisk 1866, 12). "Plain," in this respect, denotes a white "good" made ordinary and so evidently clear Fisk need not characterize it as such. Within this framework, Fisk appropriately puts the onus on Black people not to provoke "old, strong" white prejudices (18). More subtle than the "scenes of racial affective dominance" that Dwyer (2021) contends white Southern Reconstruction memoirs, history, and fiction recreate (191), pedagogical manuals like these worked much more insidiously to corresponding ends. While Fisk (1866) overtly premises his appeals as neutral—taking both the positions of formerly enslaved Black people and their former masters into account—white feelings and rationales (or internal reasoning) make invisible violences freshly experienced by his audience in favor of pleas for peaceful interdependence; the success of that interdependence relying on Black subservience to "natural" white resentment. The suffering of the past vanishes in a fugue of gaslighting magnanimity to generate white goodliness fed by Black subjection.

Despite Circumstance: From Individual Responsibility to Exceptional Example

Reconstruction pedagogical manuals offered that subjection (in varied manifestations) to its Black audience most prominently in appeals to the supposed duties that accompany "freedom"—obligations its authors conjectured as naturally immanent to it, especially as they related to Christian values. As Hartman (1997) avers, in her reading of how this material underscores the notion of "freedom" as debt and encumbrance: "Emancipation instituted indebtedness . . . The temporal attributes of indebtedness bind one to the past, since what is owed draws the past into the present, and suspend the subject between what has been and what is" (131). And, as unpacked previously, these educational props (re)construct a past that makes Black people liable for the white crimes of slavery against them. Consistently emphasized instead, the blood of war (Fisk 1866, 9; Waterbury 1864, 3) and the providence of (a Christian) God (Waterbury 1864, 3; Child 1865, 276), moreover, converge in the kindness of white people—including, allegedly, many former masters—to produce the equation that freed Black people owe much to their former captors. *Plainly* summed up, as Fisk (1866) proffers, these manuals implore their audiences to "strive to deserve the good will of all white people" (18). What Hartman (1997) calls "the burdened individuality of freedom" (130) evident in these texts arguably contributes to an educational and cultural philosophy (and eventual concatenated systems of power) predicated on ingratiating oneself to the good white nation to whom freed Black people must necessarily offer supplication based on a rescripted past: "These primers surpassed the immediate goals of a how-to book and produced a chronicle of events, a history as it were, that began the process of revision, repression, and reconciliation essential to the xenophobic and familial narrative of national identity that became dominant in the 1880s and 1890s" (131). This particular manifestation of the benevolent gaslight affords the long arc of liberal humanism a launching pad framed as "abolitionist."

Child's (1865) *The Freedmen's Book* diverts most distinctly from the optics-scrub of white violence in Fisk's (1866) and Waterbury's (1864) counsels, however. It takes on a quite different shape in that it primarily anthologizes biographical and historical sketches of Black people during slavery, with "advice" sections (authored by Child), poetry, historical notes, and other minor related ephemera spread among

　　　　　　　　　　　　　VIOLENT (RE)CONSTRUCTION(S)

those narratives throughout. The book's table of contents asterisks fifteen of its fifty-four sections as authored by eleven different Black authors—with the longest contribution of them Harriet Jacobs's and the most frequent contributor of them Frances Harper—while Child narrates most of the recounts of Black people's experiences in the remaining thirty-nine elements: These include sketches about Toussaint Louverture and Frederick Douglass, among others. In relation to contemporary readers like *The Freedman's Third Reader* (1866), *The Freedmen's Book*'s main "rival" in the genre, Karcher (1994) claims by comparison that it "strikingly illustrates how far Child had advanced beyond the concept of education that predominated in her time" (502). Historical accounts of its reception—delivered secondhand by white teachers who used the text—claim the book's graphic evocation of slave masters' and traders' brute force as "much appreciated" by its Black audience ("The Freedmen's Book" 1866, 69), with Karcher (1994) attributing to Child's text "the therapeutic function of allowing the ex-slaves to 'speak bitterness'" (503). Another Reconstruction school-teacher affirms that "an old woman who was present was so affected that she vented her feelings with a *heavy sigh*, from a heart that had ached oft on account of the evils of that 'accursed thing,' slavery" (Wilson 1870, 61–62). From the teacher's perspective, by exposing her audience to harrowing realities akin to what that audience or others around them faced, Child prompted "feeling[s] that [Black learners] have improved, not in the mere point of reading, but in thought and understanding" ("The Freedmen's Book" 1866, 69). Though white teachers read them as welcome and healing, these Black reactions could alternately denote agitation, anguish, or injury, especially given Dwyer's (2021) study of how emotions during the period operated as a tool for dominance: Heavy sighs often do not indicate appreciation. Subjection to re-traumatization so immediately relevant to the audience's lives for the purpose of goodly education aimed at advancing "the steam-car called Progress of the Colored Race" in the view of white educators (Child 1865, 276) discretely exemplifies the workings of the benevolent gaslight. These retellings undoubtedly align with, and reinforce, how whites attempted to "legally preserve the emotional politics of slavery through labour contracts" and in published historical, biographical, and fictional texts, (Dwyer 2021, 191), in tandem with their use of "the repressive instrumentality of the law . . . and orchestrated and spontaneous violence" (Hartman 1997, 140). The marked absence of white ownership of, and accountability for, slavery's violences in Reconstruction public discourse operates in concert with the deployment of accounts of that violence for coercion into a racial rehabilitation project that burdens Black shoulders with the prospects of "freedom."

Though *The Freedmen's Book* confronts the full brunt of slavery's traumas in graphic detail (ranging both Black-authored and white-authored portrayals), Child's (1865) contributions—often those particularly sketched as "advice"—regularly adopt the selfsame guilt-driven approach of Fisk and Waterbury, most evident in sections like "Advice from an Old Friend," "The Laws of Health," "Kindness to Animals," and "Education of Children." In "Advice from an Old Friend," she asserts that "being brought up as slaves, you have formed some bad habits, which it will take time to correct" (263)—the section on children's education names "lying" as one such practice (233). Following on with the point that former masters nurtured habits "still worse," she immediately qualifies that "they cannot be expected to change all at once." The abolitionist equivocates in trusting that "under the teaching of new circumstances" both groups will "improve" (263). Yet contextually specific pedagogical guidance focuses on freed Black people, gifted by do-good whites proposing moralizing self-discipline as freedom courtesy that exterior affective ruler whiteness. Indeed, "the self-appointed counselors of the freed tirelessly repeated the directive that the attainment of freedom depended on the efforts of the freed themselves" (Hartman 1997 133). Child (1865) proceeds to insinuate that Black peoples enslaved elsewhere (such as in Brazil and Spanish colonies) would directly benefit from her audience, being "sober, honest, and industrious" (270). Intrinsically, Child advocates that her freed Black addressees make themselves *the* teaching moment for the global spread of "racial" progress signaling US ethics and ideologies. The "vast amount of good" generated from subservience would depend on Black people's manners, especially in the face of openly racist whites flaunting their superiority (270). Child refers to the example of emancipated Black people in Jamaica who, in her mind, rose above the provocations of (former) slaveholders to disprove their "we-told-you-so" telos; she thus mobilizes the violence against them and their survival in spite of it as the object lesson from which US freed peoples might take heed in order to proffer another example to Portuguese and Spanish slaveholders. This racial-victimization-as-learning as consequent learning-example-for-racial-victimization cycle therefore churns on.

These burdening directives spill into Child's biographical and historical accounts as well, calling into question the communicative effects of her supposed centering of Black narratives. While rhetorician Jessica Enoch (2008) reads Child's section titled "The Beginning and Progress of Emancipation in the British West Indies" as publicizing a necessary critique of slave owners' hypocritical religious discourse (58), a closer comb of the chapter reveals rhetoric identical to that of Child's male contemporaries. The chapter operationalizes attempts at persuasion similar to Fisk (1866) and Waterbury (1864) in that Child absents white slaveholders from responsibility for the "habits" that freed Black people in Jamaica allegedly developed in slavery, in Child's case, to *specifically* compare the latter's collective behaviors post-emancipation. Individual will, a privilege absolutely denied to the enslaved, acts as a logical assumption on which the semantic construction of Child's comparison between bondage and freedom rests. She writes, "In the days of [s]lavery they herded together like animals; but now it is considered disreputable and wrong to live together without being married. In the days of [s]lavery, they wore ragged and filthy garments, but freedom has made them desirous of making a neat appearance" (1865, 145). Instead of illuminating how whites *forced* such living conditions on enslaved Black people or, more lucidly, unpacking how, according to Orlando Patterson (1982), in "powerlessness the slave became an extension of [their] master's power" in the European cultural tradition (and elsewhere) (4), Child's juxtaposition puts the onus on Black people's individual and collective willful morality to further the freedom-as-debt ethic of her peers. Child's equation affords Black people—in both enslaved and freed states—semantic agency, unlike Fisk's (1866) or Waterbury's (1864) use of the passive voice and their disappearing of grammatical subject; yet this affordance sits on a guilt-laden, gaslighting logic.

On the surface, *The Freedmen's Book* appears to present "heroic" Black protagonists in historical and contemporary narratives around slavery and freedom. One biographical sketch, that of Toussaint Louverture's role in the Haitian revolution, elicits praise from historian Butchart (2016) as a potential "source of pride" that "could provide insight into the historical roots of oppression" for Black readers (80). In comparison to the coverage of Louverture in *The Freedman's Third Reader* (1866), Butchart (2016) asserts that while the *Third Reader* absences the "duplicity" of Haitian whites, Black people's endeavors at securing their own freedom, and Black intra-racial tensions, Child's treatment shares a "stark historical drama of white supremacy on a collision course with black liberation" (79). Though Child may offer a more nuanced history than her peers by portraying some whites negatively and giving a few Black characters agency, her chapter inadvertently exemplifies a pattern repeated across many sketches throughout the book: "Good" whites facilitate the action or freedom-minded thinking of a number of Black protagonists. Child (1865) paints Louverture's "sympathetic" master, Monsieur Bayou de Libertas, as "such a humane and considerate man that life in his service seems to have been as happy as the condition of slaves can be" (37); against custom, he allowed Louverture to read (38). That concession led to Louverture drawing distinct inspiration from the writings of French Enlightenment philosopher Abbé Raynal, with Child suggesting that Louverture fulfilled Raynal's abolitionist call and prophecy of a leader of such a mission (38–39, 47). When in the service of the French army, on being named General Laveaux's second-in-command, Laveaux declares, "This is the man who Abbé Raynal foretold would rise to be the liberator of his oppressed race" (50). Even in retellings where Black figures supposedly come to the fore, white benevolence plays no small part—in fact, white desires and consolations lay the groundwork for the possibilities of what agency Black people might find in attaining their own freedoms. Child then marshals these persons and their stories of empowerment (facilitated by white "good") to frame the potential for "greatness" in "character" that "proved the capabilities" of Black people (83), in hopes that such attributes would lift her audience from their depressed social position that they just-so-happened to find themselves in due to their supposed moral ineptitude.

Elsewhere in Child's collection, benevolent enablers of Black "advancement," escape, and freedom abound in biographical stories attempting to center Black protagonists. As a child, Frederick Douglass enjoys the sympathetic graces of Mrs. Lucretia, his then-master's daughter, and later those of Mrs. Sophia Auld, "his kind mistress," who consented to his learning to read (164–165). Through an enculturation to his master's Quaker values, William Boen became "extremely temperate, scrupulously honest, and very careful never to say anything but the exact truth," and eventually his master offers him freedom (28). Whites like Baltimore merchant Elias Ellicott fueled and materially supported Benjamin Banneker's thirst for knowledge (14, 15–16). Banneker, born into freedom in 1732, "rose" out of his family's poverty with such help and subsequently gained the attention of Thomas Jefferson. Jefferson then "graciously" shared Banneker's astronomical work (without, it would seem, expressed permission) with the Academy of Sciences in Paris—Jefferson declaring in a letter to Banneker (embedded in Child's biographical sketch) that Banneker's "whole color had a right" to his scholarship as "justification against the doubts which have been entertained against them," while ironically distributing it to a white audience (20–21). Child litters the chronicle of William and Ellen Crafts's escape to/through the Northern states and afterward to England with magnanimous acts of white abolitionists, Quakers, and Northerners ensuring the couple's eventual safe passage across the pond (191–199). Mr. Crafts's "honesty, energy, and good sense" impressed the "Quakers and benevolent people, who wish to do good to Africa" along with interested merchants so much that they funded a "mission" there "important to the well-being of the world" (199–200). This mission, motivated by Crafts's desire for "elevating people of his own color," propels Child's hope that after a century Christianity's infrastructure would appear "all over Africa" (202). All through these varying examples, white kindness clears and bolsters paths through which Black success manifests as end result—in the last of them, the outcome substantiated by the possibility of tangible examples of cultural imperialism in Africa. To emphasize this assertion, Child takes a rare break from the usual third-person narrative of her biographical and historical narratives with the first person, "I hope," prefacing the colonial intent. In so doing, she drives home the grounding racializing logic of offering to freed Black people in narratives of those "like them": Cultural "advancement" travels mainly through the vehicle of "good" whites, and recounting the brutality of slavery full-throated in these narratives serves to reproduce their goodness *ad libitum.*

At play, moreover, in Child's framings of these figures and histories, the exceptional Black person—in most cases enslaved—emerges as *the* primary trope mobilized to affectively, racially, and intellectually govern her audience of freed Black learners. Child's narratives predominantly feature "intelligence" as a constituent marker funding the subsequent "freedom" and/or "success" (or possibilities thereof) for her Black protagonists. The equation's preponderance throughout *The Freedmen's Book* insinuates a link between above-average mental acumen and the propensity or suitability for living outside of bondage. Child makes that connection absolutely clear in the cases of Madison Washington, an enslaved Virginia-born man who fought his way (and coincidentally his wife's way) to safety, whom "Nature had in fact made . . . too intelligent and energetic to be contented in [s]lavery" (147); Louverture, whom Child claims as "too intelligent and thoughtful not to question in his own mind" why his *color* (rather than, tellingly, Europeans) inflicted the condition of slavery upon him (38); and the Craftses, who, likewise, "were too intelligent" not to know bondage did great "wrong" to them (181). These moments in which Child emphasizes this association couple innately with myriad other references to "intelligence" or the "intelligent" Black person—together such mentions occur over forty times throughout the book—and varying stories of Black people mostly striving their way to freedom along with other forms of social "success." Figures like Phillis Wheatley "possessed uncommon intelligence" (81); James Forten—who, born free in 1766 Pennsylvania, went on to invent and patent sailing machinery—"established a good character by his intelligence, honesty, and industry" (101–102); "Mingo," enslaved in the US South, wrote poetry eventually published in the *Boston Journal* but provoked "suspicion" with his "great intelligence" and thus made a failed attempt at escape that ended in death; and "George" (George Moses Horton), dubbed by Child "the slave poet," "early manifested remarkable intelligence" and with it attempted (unsuccessfully) to raise enough to purchase freedom through the sale of his poetry—though he did earn the respect and advocacy of the then-president of the University of North Carolina (111–113). These examples compel readers to tie freedom (or the propensity for it) with exceptional intellect.[4] At the crux of this formulation lies the assumption on its flip side—ableist, in today's parlance—that slavery inherently suits those without such "natural" or even cultured capacities. Furthermore, Child's construction of slavery for her formerly enslaved audience emphasizes to them that "freedom" (and the potentials for it) relies on exceptional aptitude to withstand the vivid violences she describes. It would seem, more pointedly, that those extraordinary subjects inherently deserve freedom more than others—a logic that continues the gaslighting guilt trip of freedom as individual/individuated burden and raises those facilitating such freedom to heroic status.

That Child, according to contemporaries as well as historians of abolition, represents *the exception* to standard Reconstruction pedagogical fare, enduring as an heroic figure through to today, seems

---

4 Elsewhere in the collection, exceptionalism takes the form of great singing talent, in the case of Ratie, "a hunchback and a dwarf with an ugly black face" (Griffith 1865, 114). Though abolitionist novelist and suffragette Mattie Griffith penned this section, it fits with Child's narratives that emphasize how Black exceptionalism prefigures possible freedom.

ironic. Butchart (2016), for example, adds only *The Freedmen's Torch-light*, New York's first Black newspaper, to Child's book as "offering images of a strong, courageous, independent black society" (80), while Enoch (2008) sets Child's apart from the American Tract Society's publications—like Fisk's (1866) and Waterbury's (1864)—as "inconsistent" with their "submissive pedagogy" (52). But the very structure and ethos of *The Freedmen's Book* propels this narrative of anomaly: Child's (1865) prefatory letter actively frames her educational reader as a "true record of what colored men have accomplished, under great disadvantages" (n.p.), as opposed to whitewashed, "sanitized" histories in *The Freedman's Third Reader* (Butchart 2016, 80) or advice books like Waterbury's (1864) and Fisk's (1866). Proclaiming selflessly "I take nothing for my services," she signals a wholly benevolent *intent* (Child 1865, n.p.), one intimately aligned with white Northern US teachers (mostly women) using her book in the US South. According to historian Jacqueline Jones (1992) in the revealingly titled *Soldiers of Love and Light*, these "[i]ntensely idealistic" teachers "embraced the rugged life and a chance to perform hard, 'useful' labor on behalf of those whom they believed were 'degraded,'" (5) a stance much in line with Child financially "roughing it" in producing the volume. Other paratextual moves, such as the semiotic identification of Black authors in her table of contents, attest to the book's driving ethic of "doing more" for those with "less"—a virtuous signaling of inclusion, solidarity, and/or coalition. With Child's voice shaping fifteen of its chapters, most of its content, and commandeering the biographical and historical narratives of ten figures and one geographic region, however, *The Freedmen's Book* forwards Child's mission. And with a careful look through the lens of the benevolent gaslight, the prevailing vision Child steers for freed Black people suggests the selfsame subjection and submission as her peers.

While insidious particularly in reconstructed narratives about Black figures, Child's (1865) guiding hermeneutic in them still primarily clings to Black freedom or "success" as motivated and enabled by white kindness, to Africa (and, of course, its racialized offspring) as in need of white Christian imperialism, even to anti-Black scientific racism that might suggest those lacking normative intelligence as fit chattel. This cloaked-as-narrative-while-interpretative conjecture manifests more conspicuously in her advice sections' wholehearted calls for deference and subservience, for turning the other cheek in spite of "much to put up with" (275) specifically contextualized by guilt-laden crediting of Lincoln, the war, and "abolitionists" who "did a great deal for you" for Black freedom (276). Her audience thus owes their future actions to those who created a system that they benefited, and continue to bene-fit, from and who perpetrated, and still perpetrate, violence (physical, emotional, intellectual, or otherwise) against said audience. Like Fisk (1866) and Waterbury (1864), Child (1865) maintains that freed Black actions should fall in line with this "reasonable" argument that "trans-parently" rules through a disciplining we-know-better-for-you-than-you logic that offers burdened individualism as "free will." In striving to demonstrate the emergence of "the post-Enlightenment European subject, the only one to enjoy the privilege of transparency" (through "scientific signifiers"), Ferreira da Silva (2007) explains that "when the racial writes Europeans and the others of Europe as subjects of exteri-ority, it institutes the body, social configurations, and global regions as signifiers of the mind" (29). The pedagogical writings analyzed herein (re)produce these signifiers in manufacturing a wholly open, giving, transparent subjectivity attempting to subject (govern) the affect-able Black other by instituting the liberal subject—as Hartman (1997) would argue. Violences of a shared past provide material scaffolding for the engineering of future sociocultural and sociopolitical control claimed finally "the steam-car called Progress of the Colored Race" (Child 1865, 276) fueled by white grace.

In Pursuit of "Goodness"

In *The Promise of Happiness*, Sarah Ahmed (2010) asks rhetorically: "How better to justify an unequal distribution of labor than to say that such labor makes people happy? How better to secure consent to unpaid or poorly paid labor than to describe such consent as the origin of good feeling?" (50). While the situation delineated by Ahmed may appear pervasive in twentieth- or twenty-first century contexts, the opposite proposition saturates Reconstruction pedagogical manuals at a cultural moment when "consent to labor" emerges as an option, at the very least a superficial one for freed Black people. These manuals, instead, promise their audience that freedom from a violent past amounts to acquiescence to a subservient (and still violent) future, that they should show gratitude for their past enslavement precisely because it shielded them from the responsibilities of free will, that they should choose to work for the same slavers (taking the moral high ground of accepting abuse when it explodes), that their agency (or lack thereof) still (forever) rests in the linger-threat of whiteness (and distinctly of whiteness wronged). That these texts purport goodly intention at a time when so many emancipated Black people in the US possessed nothing but their flesh, just recently a commodity itself, speaks to the extreme vulnerability capitalized on by this particular enactment of the benevolent gaslight.

The "goodness" of each author that this survey analyzes evades questioning altogether: Whatever personal or larger cultural motivations they carried—or left boldly pronounced in their texts—matters along with the cultural import their texts carried in their audience and the actions said import encouraged, but after all, the benevolent gaslight in whiteness's hands cares more about the *image* its users maintain as do-gooders. That image, communicated through the virtuous title of "abolitionist"—which historian James McPherson (1976) vociferously argues goes beyond emancipation's event—still lives on in current contexts as a signifier of radical political bent. But what good (of approval, of morality, but also of property) could the symbol produce in reproducing the violences from which it promises relief? An abolitionist must necessarily position themself as *against* something and that something would inherently presuppose something else worth ending. What would a white "abolitionist" of today, for instance, benefit from the dissolution of whatever system, practice, or institution of control they hope to terminate—which is to ask, otherwise: What good becomes of goodness marked through an obliteration of the liberal subject if not an argument for a "good" subject? Could that "abolitionist" function outside the paradox of the signal of self-sustaining "good" whiteness historically intrinsic in the term?

References

Ahmed, Sarah. 2010. *The Promise of Happiness*. Durham, NC: Duke University Press.

Beckles, Hilary. 1984. "Capitalism and Slavery: The Debate over Eric Williams." *Social and Economic Studies* 33 (4): 171–189.

Berkowitz, Bonnie, and Adrian Adrian Blanco. 2020. "Confederate Monuments Are Falling, but Hundreds Still Stand. Here's Where." *Washington Post*, June 17. https://www.washingtonpost.com/graphics/2020/national/confederate-monuments/.

Brinckerhoff, Isaac W. 1864. *Advice to Freedmen*. New York: American Tract Society.

Brown, Helen. 1864. *John Freeman and His Family*. Boston: American Tract Society.

Buckley, Nick (@NickBuckleyMBE). 2023. "GREAT BRITAIN ENDED THE INTERNATIONAL SLAVE TRADE. NO ONE ELSE DID IT. WE DID IT. SOME GRATITUDE IS OVERDUE." Twitter (X), August 21.

Butchart, Ronald E. 2016. "Normalizing Subordination: White Fantasies of Black Identity in Textbooks Intended for Freed Slaves in the American South, 1863–1870." In *(Re)Constructing Memory: Textbooks, Identity, Nation, and State*, edited by James H. Williams and Wendy D. Bokhorst-Heng, 73–91. Rotterdam: Sense Publishers.

Carrington, Selwyn H. H. 1984. " 'Econocide'—Myth or Reality? The Question of West Indian Decline, 1783–1806," *Boletín de Estudios Latinoamericanos y del Caribe*, no. 36: 13–48.

Chartrand, Vicki, and Justin Piché. 2019. "Abolition and Pedagogy: Reflections on Teaching a Course on Alternatives to Punishment, State Repression and Social Control." *Issues in Criminal, Social, and Restorative Justice* 22 (1): 23–42.

Child, L. Maria. 1826–1836. *Juvenile Miscellany*. Boston: Putnam & Hunt.

Child, L. Maria. 1829. *The Frugal Housewife, Dedicated to Those Who are Not Ashamed of Economy*. Boston: Carter, Hendee and Babcock.

Child, L. Maria. 1833. *An Appeal in Favor of That Class of Americans Called Africans*. Boston: Allen and Ticknor.

Child, L. Maria. 1865. *The Freedmen's Book*. Boston: Ticknor and Fields.

Clarkson, Thomas. 1808. *The History of the Rise, Progress, and Accomplishment of the Abolition of the African Slave-trade, by the British Parliament.* Vol. 1. London: James P. Parke.

Connors, Robert J. 1995. "The New Abolitionism: Toward a Historical Background." In *Reconceiving Writing, Rethinking Writing Instruction*, edited by Joseph Petraglia, 3–26. New York: Routledge.

Coupland, Reginald. (1933) 1964. *The British Anti-slavery Movement.* London: Frank Cass.

Crowley, Sharon. 1991. "A Personal Essay on Freshman English." *Pre/Text* 12: 156–176.

Drescher, Seymour. 1987. "Eric Williams: British Capitalism and British Slavery." *History and Theory* 26 (2): 180–196.

Dwyer, Erin Austin. 2021. *Mastering Emotions: Feelings, Power, and Slavery in the United States.* Philadelphia: University of Pennsylvania Press.

Engerman, Stanley L. 1972. "The Slave Trade and British Capital Formation in the Eighteenth Century: A Comment on the Williams Thesis." *Business History Review* 46 (4): 430–443.

Enoch, Jessica. 2008. *Refiguring Rhetorical Education: Women Teaching African American, Native American, and Chicano/a Students, 1865–1911.* Carbondale: Southern Illinois University Press.

Ferreira da Silva, Denise. 2007. *Toward a Global Idea of Race.* Minneapolis: University of Minnesota Press.

Fisk, Clinton B. 1866. *Plain Counsels for Freedmen: In Sixteen Brief Lectures.* Boston: American Tract Society.

The Freedman's Third Reader. 1866. Boston: American Tract Society.

"The Freedmen's Book." 1866. *The Freedmen's Record*, April 1866.

Gilbert, Helen, and Chris Tiffin, eds. *Burden or Benefit? Imperial Benevolence and Its Legacies.* Bloomington: Indiana University Press.

Goggin, Maureen Daly, and Susan Kay Miller. 2000. "What Is New About the 'New Abolitionists': Continuities and Discontinuities in the Great Debate." *Composition Studies* 28 (2): 85–112.

Griffith, Mattie. 1865. "Ratie: A True Story of a Little Hunchback" In *The Freedmen's Book*, by L. Maria Child, 114–122. Boston: Ticknor and Fields.

Hartman, Saidiya. 1997. *Scenes of Subjection: Terror, Slavery, and Self-Making in Nineteenth-Century America.* New York: Oxford University Press.

Hartman, Saidiya. 2007. *Lose Your Mother: A Journey Along the Atlantic Slave Route.* New York: Farrar, Straus and Giroux.

Hartman, Saidiya. 2019. *Wayward Lives, Beautiful Experiments: Intimate Histories of Riotous Black Girls, Troublesome Women, and Queer Radicals.* New York: W. W. Norton.

Hartman, Saidiya, and Frank Wilderson III. 2003. "The Position of the Unthought." *Qui Parle* 13 (2): 183–201.

Heuman, Gad. 1999. "The British West Indies." In *The Oxford History of the British Empire*. Vol. 3, *The Nineteenth Century*, edited by Andrew Porter and Wm. Roger Louis, 470–493. New York: Oxford University Press.

Higginson, Thomas Wentworth. 1899. *Contemporaries*. Boston: Houghton Mifflin Company.

Hopkins, Alphonso A. 1888. *The Life of Clinton Bowen Fisk. With a Brief Sketch of John A. Brooks*. New York: Funk and Wagnalls.

Jones, Jacqueline. 1992. *Soldiers of Love and Light: Northern Teachers and Georgia Blacks, 1865–1873*. Athens: University of Georgia Press.

Karcher, Carolyn L. 1994. *The First Woman in the Republic: A Cultural Biography of Lydia Maria Child*. Durham, NC: Duke University Press.

Kenschaft, Lori J. 2002. *Lydia Maria Child: The Quest for Racial Justice*. New York: Oxford University Press.

Klingberg, Frank J. 1926. *The Anti-slavery Movement in England: A Study in English Humanitarianism*. New Haven, CT: Yale University Press.

Lecky, William. 1869. *History of European Morals from Augustus to Charlemagne*. Vol. 1. New York: D. Appleton and Co.

Love, Bettina L. 2019. *We Want to Do More Than Survive: Abolitionist Teaching and the Pursuit of Educational Freedom*. Boston: Beacon Press.

Martinez, Aja Y. 2020. *Counterstory: The Rhetoric and Writing of Critical Race Theory*. Champaign, IL: National Council of Teachers of English.

M'Clintock, John, and James Strong. 1877. *Cyclopaedia of Biblical, Theological, and Ecclesiastical Literature*. Vol. 10, *Su–Z*. New York: Harper and Brothers Publishers.

McPherson, James M. 1976. *The Abolitionist Legacy: From Reconstruction to the NAACP*. Princeton, NJ: Princeton University Press.

Moland, Lydia. 2022. *Lydia Maria Child: A Radical American Life*. Chicago: University of Chicago Press.

Morgan, Kenneth. 2004. "Williams, Eric Eustace (1911–1981), Historian and Prime Minister of Trinidad and Tobago." *Oxford Dictionary of National Biography*, September 23. https://www.oxforddnb.com/view/10.1093/ref:odnb /9780198614128.001.0001/odnb-9780198614128-e-65183.

Olorunnipa, Toluse, Hannah Natanson, and Silvia Foster-Frau. 2023. "In Fight to Lead America's Future, Battle Rages over Its Racist Past." *Washington Post*, July 29. https://www.washingtonpost.com/politics/2023/07/29/fight -america-racial-history/.

Palmer, Colin A. 1994. "Introduction." In *Capitalism and Slavery*, by Eric Williams, xi–xxii. Chapel Hill, NC: University of North Carolina Press.

Patterson, Orlando. 1982. *Slavery and Social Death: A Comparative Study*. Cambridge, MA: Harvard University Press.

Rhetoric, Politics, and Culture. 2023. "Call for Papers: Rhetoric and the Abolitionist Horizon: Endings, Openings, Ruptures, Beginnings." https://msupress.org/journals/rhetoric-politics-and-culture/

Richardson, David. 1998. "The British Empire and the Atlantic Slave Trade, 1660–1807." In *The Oxford History of the British Empire*. Vol. 2, *The Eighteenth Century*, edited by P. J. Marshall, Alaine Low, and Wm. Roger Louis, 440–464. New York: Oxford University Press.

Seeley, J. R. 1883. *The Expansion of England*. London: Macmillan and Co.

Sharpe, Christina. 2016. *In the Wake: On Blackness and Being*. Durham, NC: Duke University Press.

Spillers, Hortense. 1987. "Mama's Baby, Papa's Maybe: An American Grammar Book." *Diacritics* 17 (2): 64–81.

Stock, Eugene. 1899. *The History of the Church Missionary Society: Its Environment, Its Men, and Its Work*. Vol. 1. London: Church Missionary Society.

Waite, Stacey, and Andrea Ab-Karam. 2023. " 'about to happen'/'poetry as forces': abolitionist poetics." Paper presented at Annual Convention of the Conference on College Composition and Communication, Chicago, February 17, 2023.

Ward, J. R. 1998. "The British West Indies in the Age of Abolition." In *The Oxford History of the British Empire*. Vol. 2, *The Eighteenth Century*, edited by P. J. Marshall, Alaine Low, and Wm. Roger Louis, 415–439. New York: Oxford University Press.

Warner, Ezra J. 1964. *Generals in Blue: Lives of Union Commanders*. Baton Rouge: Louisiana State University Press.

Waterbury, J. B. 1830. *Advice to a Young Christian on the Importance of Aiming at an Elevated Standard Piety by a Village Pastor*. Boston: St. John, N.B.

Waterbury, J. B. 1832. *Considerations for Young Men*. Boston: Crocker and Brewster.

Waterbury, J. B. 1838. *The Happy Christian: or, Piety the Only Foundation of True and Substantial Joy*. Boston: Crocker and Brewster.

Waterbury, J. B. 1863. *Southern Planters and Freedmen*. New York: American Tract Society.

Waterbury, J. B. 1864. *Friendly Counsels for Freedmen*. New York: American Tract Society.

Wilberforce, Robert Isaac. 1838. *The Life of William Wilberforce*. Vol. 1. London: John Murray.

Wilderson, Frank B., III. 2015. "Afro-Pessimism and the End of Redemption." Interdepartmental Seminar: Translations at John Hope Franklin Humanities Institute, Duke University, Durham, NC, October 20.

Wilderson, Frank B., III. 2020. *Afropessimism.* New York: W. W. Norton.

Williams, Eric. (1944) 1994. *Capitalism and Slavery.* Chapel Hill, NC: University of North Carolina Press.

Wilson, Joshua E. 1870. "From a Native Teacher." *The Freedmen's Record,* February.

Woodson, Carter G. (1933) 1990. *The Mis-Education of the Negro.* Trenton, NJ: Africa World Press.

Wyman-McCarthy, Matthew. 2018. "British Abolitionism and Global Empire in the Late Eighteenth Century: A Historiographic Overview." *History Compass* 16 (10): 1–12.

Yale University. 1877. *Obituary Record of Graduates of Yale University 1876/1877.* New Haven, CT: Tuttle, Morehouse, and Taylor Co.

3 · Benevolent Diversity

Student Protest and Institutional Gaslighting

In 2020, just one month before George Floyd's murder, a friend sent Black high school senior Jimmy Galligan an old Snapchat video from 2016 of their white classmate, Mimi Groves, uttering an anti-Black slur. In the video, Groves looks into the camera and says, "I can drive," followed by the N-word, expressing her excitement after receiving her learner's permit (Levin 2020). Acquiring the video four years later, Galligan thought about what to do about it. He'd heard his white classmates say the N-word before. In the past, he'd complained to teachers and administrators; often they did nothing to intervene. He decided to hold on to the video and wait. "I wanted to get her where she would understand the severity of that word," Galligan would share later (Levin 2020).

During nationwide Black Lives Matter protests after Floyd's murder a month later, Groves shared a public Instagram post urging people to "protest, donate, sign a petition, rally, do something." A stranger commented: "You have the audacity to post this, after saying the N-word" (Levin 2020). Groves panicked, quickly realizing her Snapchat video

https://doi.org/10.7330/9781646428489.c003a

from 2016 had surfaced publicly. Galligan had strategically waited until this very moment to share the video, knowing that Groves had just chosen a college to attend, committing to that university's cheer team. The video spread quickly to Snapchat, TikTok, and Twitter, sparking hundreds of emails and phone calls urging the University of Tennessee (UT)—where Groves planned to begin in the fall—to revoke her admission offer. Days later, the university cheer team ousted Groves, and pressured by admissions officials and administrators, she withdrew from the school (Levin 2020).

Despite these consequences and widespread criticism after the publicization of this news and Groves's claims of past apologies to Black friends, dozens of editorials and public opinions quickly surfaced denouncing UT's "draconian" decision not to mobilize Groves's mistake as a teaching moment (Zimmerman 2021). University of Pennsylvania professor Jonathan Zimmerman pronounced in *The Washington Post* that the university's job is "to transform students into more aware, informed, and thoughtful adults" and that it should have used "this episode" to "teach her—and, possibly, the rest of us—about human error and redemption" (Zimmerman 2021). At the same time, other editorials emerged criticizing Galligan as "vindictive" (Heitner 2021). The public dialogue circulating around Groves, UT, and Galligan importantly reveals how calls to channel Groves's mistake into a teaching moment for a white woman's future "transformation" circulate in concert with the scripting of Galligan as a cruel, angry Black man who can't "get over" Groves's past mistake. This white temporal schema disavows the immanent pain, trauma, and violence of Groves's actions, as Galligan becomes an abstract "learning object" for Groves and the particular brand of benevolent whiteness she represents in said dialogue. In scripting the timing of Galligan's reveal of the 2016 Snapchat video as rooted primarily in anger or vengeance, such a schema fails to recognize Galligan's own strategic use of *time* as a direct challenge to white futurity in a cultural/political moment that continually rebranded Floyd's death as opportunity for white teaching/learning and pedagogy. Instead, public opinion renders Galligan disruptive, malicious, and—as Zimmerman's editorial suggests—antithetical to "real" political change and growth. Even when Galligan explicitly admits his intention to "[teach] someone a lesson" in posting the video (Levin 2020), public uptake of the incident refuses to understand his temporally specific decision to reveal the video as legitimate antiracist activism or *pedagogy*, perhaps due to how it throws white progressivism, comfort, and futurity into crisis.

The example of Galligan and Groves, as well as Zimmerman's statement that UT's decision threatens the university mission to "transform students into more aware, informed, and thoughtful adults," raises the important question of why academic publics and publics writ large deem certain pedagogical acts—particularly in educational spaces—as transformative or generative with others perceived as rash, unproductive, even violent. This paradigm results from a historical and contemporary phenomenon in which racial progress remains too often contingent upon *white* recognition and futurity; any attempt at "progress" or transformation that occurs beyond the frame of white comfort or understanding signifies as merely disruptive or uncivil, even when it occurs in response to explicit racist violence and white supremacy. The ways in which universities typically respond to BIPOC faculty and students who seek to contest white supremacy both within and beyond the university exemplify this trend. Take, for instance, the case of former University of Illinois Urbana-Champaign (UIUC) American Indian studies faculty member Steven Salaita. In 2014, UIUC canceled Salaita's appointment as a tenured associate professor as a result of his impassioned tweets criticizing Israel's occupation of Palestine. Because the tweets had prompted pro-Israel alumni and donors to lobby the university to revoke Salaita's contract, the university ultimately withdrew Salaita's appointment "on the grounds that the 'tone' of his tweets against the civilian deaths and mass destruction in Gaza violated the norms of civility expected of UIUC faculty" (Trimbur 2019, 28).

As unpacked in this chapter, university power structures often weaponize the same forms of tone-policing and uneven (racialized) application of frameworks of "civility" in historical and contemporary contexts to silence and invalidate BIPOC student protest groups responding to the violences of white supremacy on campus. All too often university administrators threaten student protesters with arrest and expulsion on grounds of violating student codes of conduct (Maraj 2020, 114). The language of violation not only criminalizes student protesters but also establishes a binary that positions civil "dialogue" in a white institutional imaginary as diametrically opposed to any actions—nonviolent or otherwise—that BIPOC student protest groups take in merely responding to their own dehumanization by white institutions and actors (114). This tone-policing forwards a characteristic form of gaslighting that scripts the victims of racial violence instead as violent aggressors.

The extent of this gaslighting, especially in the university context, however, manifests as twofold: (1) it involves a renarration of present history—the idea that those who speak out in response to the violences they recently faced represent the *real* violent actors; and (2) it deploys a romanticized renarration of the *university's* history in relation to how Civil Rights and post–Civil Rights–era Black, Latinx, Indigenous, and Asian/Asian-American student protest movements critically shaped that history. Indeed, as "Benevolent Diversity" outlines, many of the identity studies programs in the contemporary university—namely, critical race/ethnic studies fields, Black studies, and women's, gender, and sexuality studies—emerged as a result of the landmark antiracist activisms of student protest groups throughout the twentieth century. Well-documented and widely known, these protestors experienced criminalization, expulsion, and violent assault for engaging in sit-ins, die-ins, and campus marches (Ferguson 2012; Kynard 2013). Half a century later, however, most universities typically embrace and romanticize these histories and movements.

Such rescripting obscures these universities' own complicity in criminalizing student protesters of color. For example, in 2018, Ohio State University celebrated the fiftieth anniversary of the 1968 Black Student Union (BSU), a group that occupied a university administrative building to protest racial inequities and anti-Black police brutality by campus police (Prasad 2022a). The group consisted of Black students who demanded greater representation of Black faculty and administrators, Black studies courses, and campus police reform after the harassment of four Black women on, and their removal from, a bus ("Ohio State Commemorates 50th Anniversary" 2018). Following the protest, a Franklin County jury indicted many of the student protesters, which led the university to implement "disruption rules" to justify expelling any students who violated them (Anderson and Oates 1998). In 2018, Ohio State invited back several BSU protest leaders, including those who had been arrested and expelled, to attend a reception with the university's then-president, Michael V. Drake, the university's first Black president. In this case, the event (and the university proper) romanticized retroactively as "real" and legitimate the Civil Rights–era student protests that inevitably led to palpable "racial progress" in the university (i.e., the university's first Black president, the creation of Black studies courses, an increase in Black faculty and administrators)—a narrative that conveniently recasts the university as historically amenable and grateful to student protesters as opposed to openly hostile and violent. How do we reconcile the university's benevolent celebration of the fifty-year anniversary of a Black student sit-in and the racial progress it necessitated with its violent treatment of mostly Black and Brown student protesters in 2016's #ReclaimOSU sit-in protest just two years prior?[1]

This chapter shows how universities, with their deep material investment and commodification of teaching, learning, and promoting civic engagement, have historically engaged—and continue to engage—a unique articulation of the benevolent gaslight that directly weaponizes

---

1 #ReclaimOSU is a divestment movement that began at Ohio State University in 2016 as a coalitional effort between Real Food OSU, United Students Against Sweatshops, Still We Rise, OSU Coalition for Black Lives, and the Committee for Justice in Palestine in an effort to bring greater transparency into the university's budget and investment information. During a sit-in protest in the OSU administrative building, Bricker Hall, on April 6, 2016, university administrators and police threatened student protesters with immediate expulsion and arrest, despite previous assurances from officials that protesters could safely occupy Bricker Hall until 5:00 a.m. the next day (Herner 2016).

"legitimate" teaching/learning to demobilize "illegitimate" racial protest. While the post-Ferguson/post-Floyd moment spurred a spike in such discourses, a simultaneous romanticization and willful misrepresentation of the Civil Rights–era and post–Civil Rights BIPOC student protest movements—primarily responsible for the university's eventual adoption of diversity and equity-oriented policies and academic initiatives—underpins this rhetorical schema. "Benevolent Diversity" highlights some of the epistemological and historical foundations of white progressivism in educational and academic spaces in showing how the university routinely sanitizes its history—especially as repeated and remembered by university administrators in response to student protests in the 20-teens—via linear, white progressive narratives surrounding historically white institutions. Specifically, the chapter spotlights the 2019 student protests at Syracuse University (SU) in response to explicit articulations of white supremacy on campus, paying particular attention to the response of SU administrators to both the racial violence on campus as well as their reactions to student protesters.

Twentieth-Century Student Protests and the Formation of Diversity and Equity Policy and Academic Initiatives

As has been well established by critical race studies, feminist and queer studies, rhetoric and writing studies, and critical university studies scholars, the US university and Western academy have long operated as an extension of state and corporate interests. Most explicitly, Melamed and Roderick Ferguson show how the academy plays these roles in the wake of World War II, a cultural and historical moment in the US when the rhetoric of minority difference and equality increasingly articulated dominant modes of power (Ferguson 2012, 7). Melamed links this phenomenon to her concept of "official antiracisms." These state-recognized antiracisms engage "liberal modes of instituting normative and rationalizing power" (Melamed 2011, 2). In so doing, they systematically validate some "orders of difference" while making others illegible

(2). Melamed locates the origins of official antiracisms in the postwar context using Howard Winant's (2001) work on the postwar "racial break." Winant characterizes the postwar racial break as "a global accumulation of sociopolitical forces—demographic, experiential, institutional, and ideological—that combined to discredit and finally undo the old world racial system" (141). Effectively, Melamed adds, the postwar moment politicized on a global scale the historical violences of white supremacy and Nazism (2011, 5), ultimately leading to a Western, US-driven "worldwide racial project, a formally antiracist, liberal-capitalist modernity that revises, partners with, and exceeds the capacities of white supremacy without replacing or ending it" (7). This landscape allowed the US to assert hegemony after the war by linking its own national race crisis to global efforts against white supremacy, ultimately lending to the creation of a kind of racial liberalism that both associates "Americanism with the benefits of capitalism" while framing the expansion of US-led global capitalism as an *antiracist* project (10).

In this postwar context, Ferguson explains, state, capital, and the academy/university thus "began to see minority difference and culture as positivities that could be part of their own 'series of aims and objectives,'" articulating a situation whereby dominant institutions could "reduce the initiatives of oppositional movements to the terms of hegemony" (Ferguson 2012, 6–7). This script provided fertile grounds for technologizing the benevolent gaslight by renarrating anti-institutionality as institutional capital. Eventually, by the 1980s, as the state began to shrink federal support from social services and higher education post–Civil Rights and Black Power movements, debates surrounding "the importance of the liberal arts versus the necessity of managerial training" led to what Lisa Duggan (2012, 10) calls a "new liberalism" that combined pro-market, pro-business attitudes with the "shrunken remnants of social democratic and social justice programs of Western welfare states." This prompted a kind of twenty-first-century multicultural neoliberal "'equality' politics" in dominant cultural, political, and educational institutions.

　　　　

While many humanities scholars now commonly critique the university as a neoliberal institution (Ahmed 2012, Melamed 2011, Riedner and Mahoney 2008), Ferguson suggests that student movements and their histories enable us to understand university neoliberal paradigms and their "flow of influence" (2012, 9) more specifically in relation to antiracist rhetorics and movements. The diverse social formations within the university expressed by US student movements, he avers, suggest that "the academy is not simply an entity that socializes people into ideologies of political economy," but rather an institution that critically *socializes* state and capital "into emergent articulations of difference" (9). In other words, the academy does not merely reflect state interests but also serves as a primary "articulator" of the state's management of power and, specifically, minority difference (11). For this reason, the student movements of the 1960s and 1970s that helped the university devise its distinct lexicon for benevolently managing (racial) difference provided ample opportunity for the university to extend its own geopolitical project while appearing on the surface to disrupt it in the name of progress (11). Ferguson's historicization here makes visible how these social movements and the formation of the interdisciplines as well as the diversity/inclusion initiatives that emerged from them helped establish a discursive and material foundation for the benevolent gaslight: Institutional, racialized power worked "through the 'recognition' of minoritized histories, cultures, and experiences" while subsequently using that very same "recognition" to "resecure its status" (13). In turn, the work of student movements and the historical circumstances they reflect geared the academy to operate as a "training ground" for state and capital's engagement with minority difference (11).

As an illustrative case study, Ferguson discusses the Lumumba-Zapata student movement at the University of California San Diego (USCD), which took place from 1969 to 1972. Against a backdrop of milestone student protests like the Third World Liberation Front strikes at universities like San Francisco State and UC Berkeley in the late 1960s,[2] Black and Chicanx students at UCSD—including Angela Davis, then a graduate student—organized in 1969 to propose the creation of a new "third" college at UCSD that would be named Lumumba-Zapata College after the assassinated Congolese revolutionary Patrice Lumumba as well as the Mexican revolutionary Emiliano Zapata (Ferguson 2012, 43). Lumumba-Zapata organizers sought to deepen and broaden "minority difference's relationship to political and institutional practice by creating a college expressly devoted to the needs of students from oppressed social groups" (52). As such, UCSD Lumumba-Zapata students put together a curriculum reflecting their interests. They called, for example, for the inclusion of authors like Malcolm X, Kwame Nkrumah, Frantz Fanon, George Padmore, Che Guevara, and Mariano Auzela and the creation of a curriculum structured by the following categories: "Revolutions," "Analysis of Economic System," "Science and Technology," "Health Sciences and Public Health," "Urban and Rural Development," "Communication Arts," "Foreign Languages," "Cultural Heritage," and "White Studies" (53).

However, despite Lumumba-Zapata organizers' attempts to radically oppose the academy's relationship to state, capital, and racial hegemony, Ferguson notes, "a new strategic situation was developing that would attempt to turn the critiques of the student movements into hegemonic maneuvers of American institutions" (67). UCSD administrators attempted to "drive a wedge" in the coalition between Black and Chicanx students by appointing administrators touting Black nationalist rhetorics that ignored the exclusion of Chicanx students in recruitment and hiring, and the university began generally limiting the recruitment of underrepresented students, actions that would ensure the new third college "would be 60 percent white by 1976" (74). These

---

2 The Third World Liberation Front (TWLF) emerged in 1968 as a cross-racial coalitional movement involving Black, Latinx, Indigenous, and Asian/Asian-American student protesters calling for a decentering of white, Eurocentric disciplines and education in US universities. The TWLF played a central role in the eventual establishment of ethnic studies and identity studies fields across US universities, beginning with the first College of Ethnic Studies at San Francisco State and the Ethnic Studies Department at the University of California, Berkeley. See Dong (2009) for a more detailed discussion of these protests and their impacts.

localized actions undertaken by UCSD, Ferguson asserts, exemplify shifts in broader mechanisms of power in order to "manage insurgent articulations of minority difference, without absolute suppression but through selective revision and deployment" (75). Lumumba-Zapata might therefore read as "a chronicle of how minority difference was deployed against institutional hegemony," yet subsequently "claimed by and managed within the province of institutions" in ways that alienated it from its original mission (75).

Accordingly, UCSD named the eventual "third" college it formed not Lumumba-Zapata College but instead Third College, a name since changed to Thurgood Marshall College after the first Black US Supreme Court justice, Thurgood Marshall. Even in the college's naming, UCSD strategically manages the college's more radical history. The erasure of "Lumumba-Zapata" in favor of an homage to Thurgood Marshall celebrates a particular "legitimate" model of minority difference that upholds state representatives and actors over the anti-state radical revolutionaries that initially inspired the college's formation. Not surprisingly, UCSD's own dominant remembering calculatedly sanitizes Thurgood Marshall College's history. The "About Thurgood Marshall College" page on UCSD's website (as of 2024) describes its founding in 1970 as occurring "in a period of transformative social change in the United States and the world" (UC San Diego 2024)—rather than principally motivated by radical activisms of Black and Chicanx students.

US universities' cleansing of radical racial histories, as in the case of Thurgood Marshall College, does more than rescript the past. Importantly, as a mechanism of the benevolent gaslight, it also disciplines present and even *future* student movements' endeavors by ensuring that current and ongoing violence or erasure registers as individualized, exceptional phenomena rather than products of a historical continuum. As many postcolonial studies scholars establish, colonial and white supremacist power structures continue to intentionally perpetuate their control through disbarring comprehensive access to one's history. Consider, for instance, the British Empire's well-documented and intentional destruction of past historical records evidencing the use of torture in Africa and Asia.[3] The British government has often justified the concealment and destruction of these historical records by claiming them hidden by "mistake," a narrative that, as some historians maintain, implicitly emphasizes colonizers' ongoing desire to "avoid reputational embarrassment" (Linebaugh 2022, 732). Such reframings suggest that colonial fragility and the white desire to appear "good" did not recede upon "decolonization." White benevolence, in other words, has long operated as a white supremacist and colonial mechanism to rationalize historical misrepresentation. US universities' rose-colored renarrations of radical racial unrest represent just one of many mechanisms that mobilize and reinforce white dominance and "ownership" of history.

In the specific context of US universities, however, such historical misrepresentations often occur through a kind of romanticization and pro-institutional nostalgia surrounding Civil Rights–era activisms that tactically misremember the embodied disruption intentionally deployed by counter-institutional student protesters in the past to police protest and disruption that occur in the *present* and even *future*. As the next section illustrates, this narrative enables universities to operationalize the benevolent gaslight in positioning themselves as "officially antiracist" (Melamed 2011, 2) while subsequently rendering the antiracist pedagogies of BIPOC student movements unrecognizable, illegitimate, and hostile to "real" racial progress.

---

3 As an extreme example, one might think of the infamous 2011 Hanslope Park Disclosure's "migrated archives," files that documented British colonizers' systemic use of torture in Kenyan detention camps that, upon the eve of Kenya's declaration of independence from British rule in 1963, were quietly transferred from Kenya to England for "safe keeping on account of their historical value," as Kenya's final colonial Governor MacDonald attested (Linebaugh 2022, 735). These "migrated archives" notably corroborated survivors of the Mau Mau rebellion's testimonies surrounding the British's usage of torture in a 2011 lawsuit against the UK government (731). As a result of the publicity crisis these recently declassified files engendered, the UK Foreign and Commonwealth Office (FCO) claimed, interestingly, that the colonial records "were hidden by mistake," even though it ultimately became clear that the concealment had been primarily motivated by a "desire to avoid reputational embarrassment" (732).

#NotAgainSU

In November 2019, Syracuse University (SU) reported over a dozen racist and anti-Semitic graffiti and assaults over the course of just two weeks. This particular spike in racist incidents began on November 7, when racist vandalism was first reported in freshman residence halls. Five days later SU announced publicly the discovery of the racist graffiti, which was followed two days later by the appearance of anti-Asian racist graffiti in SU's Day Hall. Between November 16 and 18, the momentum picked up: Additional racist graffiti and swastikas were found in campus buildings, white students were reported to be yelling anti-Back slurs, members of the SU campus community received a "hateful email," a Black woman was called the N-word as she walked past the Alpha Chi Rho frat house, and an unknown person attempted to share a white supremacist manifesto via Apple's AirDrop function with students at SU's Bird Library. As of November 21, several additional incidents had been reported, including even more anti-Black, anti-Indigenous, and anti-Asian graffiti across three campus buildings (Weaver 2019).

In the midst of these racist acts on campus, student protesters—largely BIPOC students and some white allies—formed a coalition by the name of "#NotAgainSU." By November 13, #NotAgainSU—as well as, later on, members of the local NAACP—gathered to stage a multiday, twenty-four-hour sit-in at the SU Barnes Center to protest the university's inadequate responses to the incidents (Anderson 2019). Additionally, #NotAgainSU, along with a coalition of international students, issued a list of nineteen demands to SU white Chancellor Kent Syverud, "which included clarifying the student code of conduct to explicitly include elevated punishments for acts of racism, developing a facility to house multicultural student resources and forming mandatory diversity and inclusion curriculum and training for all faculty and staff, with input from students and faculty members of color" (Anderson 2019).[4] They also called for Syverud's resignation.

---

4 Importantly, SU ultimately did not commit to meeting all of #NotAgainSU's demands, though they did commit to "98 percent" of them (McMahon 2019). Syverud made

Importantly, #NotAgainSU organizers emphasized, the systemic failures of the SU administration to address racism on campus spanned beyond these two weeks in November 2019. Indeed, as Ferguson reminds us, students of color at historically white institutions have attested to the widespread culture of indifference to explicit and implicit racisms on campus since the 1970s (Anderson 2019).

In the specific purview of the SU protests, the institutional rhetorics mobilized by campus representatives and administrators in response to student protesters engage in benevolent gaslighting on four levels: (1) by renarrating both the racist incidents and student protesters' organizing as a teaching/learning moment for the university; (2) by spectacularizing racist acts as exceptional instances threatening the "progress" made since the Civil Rights era rather than as events along a historical continuum; (3) by redirecting blame toward "destructive" or "violent" student protesters who seemingly threaten the racial harmony of the benevolent, teaching/learning–centered university; and (4) by mobilizing fictitious claims to "antiracist" ethos through a romanticization and misrepresentation of the university's own history as an institution influenced by the radical activisms of Black, Latinx, Indigenous, and Asian/Asian-American student movements.

Syverud's public response to #NotAgainSU's demands in a November 20, 2019, press conference proves especially revealing. In the first part of his public address, Syverud begins by narrating a timeline of the incidents that led to the #NotAgainSU protests. He emphasizes the SU administration and police department's belief that primarily one to five members of the community carried out the acts, reassuring the audience of the police's "more than full-time" work to determine the identities of

---

particular revisions to some of the demands, stating that legal requirements and Board of Trustees policies made it difficult to ensure that all demands could be met. Legal requirements, for example, made it impossible for SU to ensure racial identity could be considered as a factor in roommate selection (a demand made by #NotAgainSU). Syverud also noted that the status of tenured professors' training in diversity could only be shared "up to the extent of the law," though he did commit to make diversity training required for tenure (McMahon 2019). He also stated that he would "strongly urge" the Board of Trustees to meet with students twice a year (McMahon 2019). See McMahon (2019) for a full list of #NotAgainSU's original demands.

  BENEVOLENT DIVERSITY

the one to five individuals. Later, he adds greater context to the previously reported incident of the Black woman student verbally accosted outside the Alpha Chi Rho frat, highlighting that of the fourteen people involved in the incident, only four were actually students at SU. Of the ten from other universities—allegedly the primarily offenders—he claims the "most aggressive" student as affiliated with Rutgers University (Syverud 2019). Finally, he describes the events at Bird Library where someone attempted to AirDrop a white supremacist manifesto to students in the vicinity. Despite the "immediate fear" and "chaos" among students that the incident sparked, he characterizes the reports of the incident as "probably a hoax"; law enforcement, he shares, "has not been able to locate a single person" in possession of the white supremacist manifesto. Nonetheless, Syverud reiterates that such racisms at SU pose an "immediate challenge to our institutions and its values" (Syverud 2019).

Even in Syverud's seemingly "objective" timeline of events, he enacts a series of distancing moves meant to deflect blame away from both the SU administrators as well as SU's "values" as an institution. Clint G. Graves and Leland G. Spencer (2022, 58) refer to this shifting and distancing of blame as an "ethotic" form of racialized gaslighting, not entirely unlike the ways in which state discourses typically engage in blaming rhetorics that criminalize Black people killed or assaulted by police in order to reframe the violence as legally justified or necessary. Ethotic forms of racialized gaslighting, in other words, minimize the violences or negligence the perpetrating institution enacts by reasserting the institution's apparently just and blameless ethos. Syverud's many attempts to create distance from or minimize SU's complicity in the events that took place exemplify this reassertion, as he often uses numerical appeals that rhetorically diminish the involvement of SU. By spotlighting *only* one to five students as culpable for the racist acts and *only* four of the fourteen students who verbally assaulted the Black female student as affiliated with SU, Syverud strives to cast off any suspicion that a broader culture of white supremacy at SU enabled such on-campus racisms. In fact, Syverud frames these racisms as a *threat* to the university since they pose an "immediate challenge to our institution and its values" (Syverud 2019).

In addition to his ethotic, racialized gaslighting, this personification of the institution as the *legitimate* victim functions, Sara Ahmed illuminates, as a prototypical vehicle of institutional racism. This narrative casts the institution as "the subject of feeling, as the one who must be protected, as the one who is easily bruised or hurt" (Ahmed 2012, 147), often at the expense of the Black, Indigenous, Asian/Asian-American, and Jewish students, faculty, and staff hurt or made unsafe as a result of SU's inaction. Syverud's conclusion, then, that marks the incident at Bird Library a "hoax" assumes a binary between "legitimate" and "illegitimate" evidence: the former characterized by law enforcement/police with the latter assumed as fearful and "chaotic" students' anecdotal reports. This structural delegitimization of students' embodied and experiential narratives evinces racialized gaslighting's "failure to yield epistemic ground" to people of color (Graves and Spencer 2022, 58). It also establishes a foundation for the university to renegotiate how these racialized incidents are documented and remembered in the official narrative.

While Graves and Spencer help illustrate how Syverud engages rhetorics that constitute racial gaslighting, their framework of racialized gaslighting does not fully account for what comes in the second part of the public address. Following his remark about the institution's values, Syverud briefly laments what he perceives as an emergent "acceptable leadership style" of ignoring facts and attacking people (Syverud 2019)—a statement both strategically ambiguous and politically expedient—as he never specifically names whom or what he critiques: Is this about Trump? The perceived aggression of student protesters? The racist perpetrators at SU? Then, stunningly, Syverud shifts to a personal appeal: "That's not who I am or how I was raised" (Syverud 2019). He goes on to discuss his many past conversations with students and faculty of color on campus, stating that they asked repeatedly whether "he can ever understand how miserable and unacceptable" experiencing such violent racisms in one's place of schooling or work could be. He responds by sharing that he *can* understand these experiences, since he spent "6 years of [his] life" fighting for race-based affirmative action in the South while raising a mixed-race family. In depicting the traumas of his own racialized family as pedagogical fodder, he emphasizes that "[his] kids were threatened," his wife "was subjected to many racial epithets," his family's "car tires were slashed," and, fighting back tears, he adds, his kids' "dog was shot." He concludes this narrative by pronouncing "that was then. That was the South. But this is Syracuse. This is 2019. I do not accept this hatred here and now" (Syverud 2019). Shifting strategically now to passive voice, Syverud admits that things "have not been handled well enough . . . were not communicated well enough." We "have learned a lot from these instances," he attests, "but not enough yet" (Syverud 2019). Here Syverud not only rebrands the 2019 racist incidents as teaching/learning opportunity, but he also endeavors to distance himself from complicity with SU's mishandling of racist offenses by reasserting a kind of antiracist ethos and presumably long-held commitment to racial equity via both the oppressions his mixed-race family faced as well as the "6 years of [his] life" he spent fighting for race-based affirmative action.

This move importantly technologizes a *benevolent* gaslight as it evinces Syverud's shift from guilt/blame to benevolent, antiracist pedagogue: Not only has his commitment to antiracism as a white man with the best of intentions existed *perennially*, but his lesson "learned" rests yet again on the backs of SU students, staff, and faculty of color in 2019 in addition to his own racialized family's traumas. However, his implicit romanticization of both the racisms and racial movements of the past foregrounds another key element of Syverud's appeals here. By emphasizing his own work on behalf of civil rights during an era of "real" racism in the South, he invests in a (white) narrative of linear, liberal progress. Because of the *real* resistance work that happened in the past in response to *real* racisms, in 2019 in Syracuse things work differently "here" and "now": Contemporaneous racist acts represent mere aberrations from the institution's "values"; the institution does not directly enable, facilitate, or commit them.

Syverud also manifests here another significant feature of the benevolent gaslight's temporality: the white weaponization of romanticized racial progress narratives surrounding the Civil Rights movement as a mode of invalidating the racial present. Critical race theorists often refer to such romanticized post–Civil Rights memories as "master narratives" (Ladson-Billings and Tate 1995, Solórzano and Yosso 2002). These (white) social mythologies "mute, erase, and neutralize features of racial struggle in ways that reinforce ideologies of White supremacy" (Woodson 2017, 317). As Ashley N. Woodson (2017) underlines, Civil Rights master narratives typically buttress white supremacy in four key ways: (1) by essentializing Black people and Black struggle; (2) by portraying racism as an accident or aberration; (3) by reinforcing stories of singular martyrs or messiahs; and (4) by suggesting that the Civil Rights movement eliminated racism (320). In such frames, because past struggles for racial equality eliminated structural racism and "real" white supremacy, contemporary racial struggles or violences read as deviations from, or even as *threats* to, the norm (322). By invoking his past experiences as an ethotic appeal, Syverud reasserts a white master narrative in which he implicitly positions himself as a kind of martyr or messiah as a result of both his own work on behalf of racial equity and civil rights during at time of "real" racism as well as his association with his Black wife and mixed-race children. This scripting demonstrates the benevolent gaslight's deflecting of blame via a performance of white progressivism.

Rather than a specific aspect of Syverud's rhetoric, this romanticized master narrative of racial progress in the context of institutions of higher education serves as a central feature of how US universities understand and narrate their histories post–Civil Rights. Similar appeals pervade other examples already discussed, such as UCSD's Thurgood Marshall College and OSU's celebration of the fiftieth anniversary of the 1968 Black Student Union. Each of these cases illustrates how essentialized "official antiracisms" of white master narratives

           BENEVOLENT DIVERSITY

systematically and retroactively recuperate into the abstract the radical histories of Black, Indigenous, Latinx, and Asian/Asian-American student resistance and activism in the university. This phenomenon also enacts what Eli Meyerhoff (2019, 5) calls "the education romance" whereby US universities might embrace "romantic stories about education" and, by implication, the university itself, that obscure and make impossible material interventions into universities' ongoing racialized and gendered carceral regimes.

Such racial progress "master" narratives deployed in/by the university also benevolently gaslight by neutralizing and tone-policing antiracist student movements such that conversations surrounding protest become mainly focused on the mode of protest as opposed to the material demands of protesters or the racisms that initially sparked protests. Unsurprisingly, then, Syverud—following his statement that "we have learned a lot from these instances"—ends his public address by emphasizing the importance of being "careful and graceful" in how "we" respond, as "we will be judged not on what these hateful people do to us, but how we respond to it." Such grace and care become necessary to avoid being "controlled by these hateful people" (Syverud 2019). This tone-policing, "focusing on the emotion behind the message rather than the message itself," acts as a crucial element of racial gaslighting as well as a pivotal factor often inhibiting effective cross-racial communication (Davis and Ernst 2019, 49). By implicitly shifting blame from "hateful people" to what he suggests as the careless/graceless response by protesters, Syverud also evinces what some scholars in communication studies term the "protest paradigm" (Brown and Mourão 2022, 739). This paradigm describes the tendency of dominant, whitestream cultural and political narratives to assume that antiracist protesters have a greater "penchant for engaging in criminality and disruption" (Brown and Mourão 2022, 739), a characterization based in racialized, gendered, and classed assumptions about BIPOC people's particular tendencies toward anger or irrationality (Cherry 2021, Lin et al. 2006, Palmer 2017). This scripting also relies on a kind of white exceptionalism that historically celebrates or admires instances of violent or unruly property destruction by whites like the Boston Tea Party—or even Syverud's own past work of advocating for race-based affirmative action—while deeming the anger of #NotAgainSU protesters uncivil, overly emotional, or lacking grace. Syverud's own display of tearful emotion even further reinforces this idea. Emotion, one might assume, functions as acceptable when embodied by benevolent whites who represent the institution but perhaps not when felt and performed by student protesters of color.

The Romance of Education and the Benevolent Gaslight

The implied valorization of rational, "graceful" discourse by US universities forwards a linear (white) temporality and suggests rational, moral persuasion as a solution to educational and cultural crises (Meyerhoff 2019, 48). This "romance of education," Meyerhoff explains, bolsters a "romantic story of a heroic individual climbing the educational ladder higher and higher, while overcoming obstacles at each rung, toward the good life—to success, security, autonomy, independence, maturity, and happiness" (43). It thus treats educational modes of study as inherently progressive while neglecting "alternative modes of study" of the institution that might disrupt these progressivist narratives (48). As a means of dominant institutional worldmaking complicit with capitalist, white supremacist, and colonial logics and structures, the romance of education leaves little room for other critical genealogies of universities and disciplines that divest from "politically neutral, 'objective' history" in favor of a deep analysis of the political conditions out of which particular objects of study emerged (200). One might easily apprehend, then, how the benevolent gaslight's embrace of the teaching/learning moment, too, fits within the schema of the romance of education: The reframing of institutionally enabled racial violence as fodder for white teaching/learning renders racial violence a necessary component of the "educational ladder" (43). This imaginary makes it nearly impossible to unsettle or critique the university's own complicity with white supremacist logics and

　　　　BENEVOLENT DIVERSITY

histories, for racial violence serves as the capital invested in perpetuity for racial "progress."

Education, Meyerhoff reminds us, "is just one possible mode of study among many alternatives" (2019, 4). In other words, just as dominant methods of knowledge-making offer "world-making" projects (4), so too do the critical genealogies of the institution mobilized by antiracist student protest groups like #NotAgainSU who articulate alternative visions of universities and their histories.[5] Indeed, even in the name "#NotAgainSU," the phrasing "not again" suggests both a historical critique of ongoing institutional passivity as well as an implied call to imagine SU differently. By physically occupying campus buildings, disrupting and inhibiting "business as usual," and forcing white institutional intervention, sit-ins by BIPOC students reference and continue a much longer history. Historian Deidre Flowers (2005) notes, for example, the dominant use of sit-ins as a Civil Rights–era practice mobilized by Black students protesting school segregation in the 1960s, though the practice itself might date back to the Reconstruction era (55). Sit-ins, Flowers shares, challenge white supremacist logics meant both literally and figuratively to keep Black people "in their place" (60). Among many other tactics, sit-ins also functioned as a central practice during influential nationwide student protests in the late 1960s, such as the San Francisco State College Third World Liberation Front, a movement led by Black, Asian-American, Latinx, and Indigenous students demanding the establishment of ethnic studies and open admissions (Rojas 2010, Soldatenko 2022, Umemoto 1989).

Moreover, Kynard reads contemporary Black student protest as *the* history of contemporary US higher education itself. In discussing 2015 protests at the University of Missouri (MU),[6] Kynard (2018, 524) draws

---

5 See Prasad (2022a) for an extended discussion of antiracist student protest as university world-making.

6 In September and October 2015, MU students organized on campus as part of the "Racism Lives Here" movement to protest unaddressed incidents of racism on campus. In response to then-MU President Tim Wolfe's inaction, Jonathan L. Butler, a Black graduate student, engaged in a hunger strike calling for Wolfe's resignation (Miller 2015). Wolfe did finally resign, but only after MU football players refused to play or practice in solidarity with Butler. Out of fear of financial loss as a result of

attention to the ways Black queer student protesters—like Payton Head, a former MU student body president and activist—"signal the semiotics" of Black protest movements and moments, mobilizing race-radical literacies to communicate with (counter)public audiences "in ways that draw on long-standing protest traditions and Black vernacular processes that have continually repurposed colleges." She locates these activist literacies as part of a long tradition throughout the twentieth and twenty-first centuries that began as early as the 1920s at Black colleges like Fisk University and sustained through Civil Rights–era student movements like the 1960s Student Non-Violent Coordinating Committee (SNCC) and into the post-Ferguson moment. Black insurgency on college campuses, Kynard advances, "draws upon a century-old literacy tradition that merges community protests, vernacular expressivity, new aesthetics, new information technologies, and new diasporic migrations." This history "shows us that an anti-racist campus culture and knowledge system is a fundamental human right and guiding purpose of education" (525). Kynard frames this particular history of higher education as "foundational"; it requires grasping Black protest, race resistance, and counterpublic discursive creativity "as central to what it means to do literacy in American colleges" (525).

#NotAgainSU's intentional mobilization of these historically situated, embodied race-radical literacies both directly and indirectly articulate an alternative history of the university as an institution whose ability to perform a vision of racial "progress" owes much to the historical work of Black, Latinx, Indigenous, and Asian/Asian-American student movements, even if benevolent white rhetorics and logics routinely sanitize, make invisible, or discipline these histories. Paying heed to how universities carry out such maneuvers need not, however, provide a kind of antidote or blueprint for "corrective" replication of these race-making literacies—as the benevolent gaslight often depends on disorienting extraction. As Ferguson illuminates in his later project, *We Demand: The University and Student Protests* (2017),

the MU football players' strike, Wolfe resigned in November 2015 (Tarlep and Belkin 2015).

 BENEVOLENT DIVERSITY

the radical manifestos deployed by student movements across the US in the 1960s and 1970s insisting on "the reorganization of institutional life *and* the reorganization of knowledge on college campuses" threw US government and university administration into crisis, forcing them to determine methods for how to "best manage the progress and direction of the university" (Ferguson 2017, 17). Universities, in fact, deployed the category of "diversity" in opposition to students of color "and their visions of social justice" (17). Ferguson links this campaign to the policies and rhetorics of then-President Richard Nixon, who established the President's Commission on Campus Unrest in response to contemporaneous killings at Kent State and Jackson State of student activists of color.[7] The resulting *Report of the President's Commission on Campus Unrest* worked to construct students as potential criminals disrupting the social order (18). Ferguson highlights that the report's criminalization of students performs a "sleight of hand"—a kind of *gaslight*—by framing student activists as "threats to democracy rather than as people whose freedoms should have been protected under democratic law" (18). Nixon's broader rhetorical appeals throughout his presidency buttress this assertion, as they often repurposed the language of "civil rights" to snuff out racial unrest and preserve the white social order (19).

The consequent push for diversity initiatives in universities, then, that extends into the post-Ferguson moment has long functioned to rebrand student movements as "occasions to clarify the 'essential function' of the university for liberal democracy" (Ferguson 2017, 24). As Nixon's report lays out, homogeneity and awareness around "values held in common"

---

7   In April 1970, Kent State University students in Ohio organized to protest the US invasion of Cambodia, the deaths of US soldiers, and the recent killings of Vietnamese civilians. Students also, importantly, were protesting the draft, which largely led to the selection of young men from economically and racially disenfranchised backgrounds (Ferguson 2017, 14). By May, the National Guard had been dispatched to Kent State to forcibly end protests, ultimately leading to the deaths of four people—Jeffrey Glen Miller, Allison B. Krause, William Knox Schroeder, and Sandra Lee Scheuer—as well as the wounding of nine others (15). By mid-May, protests had also broken out at Jackson State University in Jackson, Mississippi (a historically Black university). Local police riddled a women's dorm with bullets, and two Black men—Philip L. Gibbs and James Earl Green—were killed (15).

in the post–Civil Rights university became a way of fusing diversity with "the nation's health," a project that led to the "creation of a stratum of intellectuals who would use diversity to manage conflict in the student body in the name of the life of the campus and health of the nation" (24). (Syverud's framing of the 2019 SU incidents as threats to the university's values comes to mind here.) Racial identities—consequent to Nixon's report and its legacy—act as "resources" for, rather than hinderances to, university administrators' "efforts to manage activism and conflict" (25). Furthermore, framing students as "figures of disorder" reduces student protesters' demands to "personal grievances" that simple bureaucratic interventions like faculty hiring, inclusive/diverse student admissions, and alternative modes of curricular development might manage (26). These initiatives produce a kind of paradox for BIPOC students and laborers in historically white institutions. In the words of Lisa Lowe (1998, 41), though the institutionalization of diversity initiatives and disciplines like ethnic studies provides "a material base within the university for a transformative critique of traditional disciplines," it remains the case that "the institutionalization of any field or curriculum that establishes orthodox objects and methods submits in part to the demands of the university and its educative function of socializing subjects into the state." Indeed, the disciplinary orientation in critical race studies that makes this book possible ironically itself represents a product of this institutionalization.

These histories, as well as the recent example of SU, demonstrate how US colleges and universities have played, and still continue to play, an essential role in perpetuating the romance of education that vitally underpins and legitimizes the benevolent gaslight. More than individualized acts carried out by bad-apple whites, the benevolent gaslight operates as a structural force, deeply embedded in the way institutions of higher education manage, negotiate, and tame, especially in response to moments that threaten whitestream, sanitized histories. Benevolent gaslighting, as a way of managing time and memory, fabricates and weaponizes revisionist histories to "dictate the pace of racial progress" (Cooper 2016, n.p.) as a technology of white time. It disavows the ways racial violences—as well as the antiracist resistance acts and movements that seek to respond to them—reconstitute white imaginaries of progress and closure in pointing to a nonlinear continuity of racism (Ore and Houdek 2020, 444).

#NotAgainSU's implicit and explicit suggestions that SU's culture of white supremacy never ended critically interrupt white time's racial forgetting in adopting an "alternative temporal orientation" or, as Ersula Ore and Matthew Houdek term it, a "countertemporality" that facilitates "different forms of meaning-making, memory, and justice" (Ore and Houdek 2020, 452). Ore and Houdek—in their discussion of the rhetorical power of recognizing the deaths of Emmett Till, Trayvon Martin, and Michael Brown as instances of lynching and therefore part of the *same* prolonged moment—assert that such countertemporalities that "reimagine the present as an accumulation and intensification of the past" expose how "Black disposability has historically served the nation" and "constituted white democratic citizenship" (452). While the SU incidents and others like it across history manifest differently from the lynchings of Till, Martin, and Brown, similar temporal logics fund the university's management of student protesters. As evident in end-of-lynching discourse, Syverud's moves to distance both the past from the present, and SU from racist violence, reflect "an ongoing tradition to rhetorically save face" (Ore 2019, 6), to produce and sustain white "law and public memory" (Ore and Houdek 2020, 445), and to depict extreme racial violence and white supremacy as singular or isolated events (445). Statements like "that was then. That was the South. But this is Syracuse. This is 2019," like end-of-lynching discourses, offer up a sense of time (and space) that "appears as common sense" (445). University administrators thus recast student protesters' mobilization of alternative temporal orientation to white supremacist racism across the twentieth and twenty-first centuries as deeply unhealthy, lacking "grace," and detrimental to the institution. This reframing thwarts how these protestors' tactics reveal the centrality of racial violence and "Black disposability" to US nationalism/democratic citizenship (Ore and Houdek 2020, 452), global capitalism, and "worldwide racial project[s]" (Melamed 2011, 7) that have long been materialized through and by US universities and their representatives (Ferguson 2012, 9). The manipulation of racialized time, then, sustains the benevolence of the liberal university.

Conclusion

The radical histories of Black, Indigenous, Latinx, and Asian/Asian-American student protest that ultimately led to the widespread creation of diversity initiatives and identity studies departments at US universities do not sit in tension with recent examples like SU in 2019 as a matter of accident, exception, or coincidence. In sanitizing and romanticizing histories of racial unrest in ways that valorize white, linear progress narratives and institutional logics, US universities sustain their historical participation in a broader geopolitical and imperialist state project of managing minoritized difference and racial disruption. To do so, these institutions weaponize a range of benevolent rhetorics of teaching/learning: the formation of identity studies disciplines; the strategic use of "diversity" initiatives as a Nixon-era strategy of snuffing out racial insurrection; and the reframing of higher education as a "formally antiracist" project (Melamed 2011, 7) that portrays anti-institutional critiques that might threaten white dominance as antithetical to "real" racial progress—all moves that Syverud and many others like him make. In this articulation of the benevolent gaslight, progressivist narratives of teaching/learning render racial progress or even the acknowledgment of racism's existence contingent upon *white* institutional recognition and validation. These narratives strategically misrepresent the radical histories of resistance that foundationally shaped universities; they discipline, alienate, and gaslight the historical and ongoing race-radical literacies forwarded by movements like #NotAgainSU or even individual resistance acts like Galligan's temporally strategic exposure of his white classmate's racism.

In demonstrating some of the principal modes through which US universities benevolently gaslight student protest and resistance acts, the examples of SU and Syverud emphasize the importance of historical revisionism—the act of "leaving behind and moving on" (Ngo 2019, 245)—to the project of white supremacy and dominance. These violences do not just play out discursively or epistemologically. They also manifest as physically or psychically cruel. Recall the recent example of the University of Kansas (KU), which, in September 2022, passively reported that "it has come to [their] attention" (Girod et al. 2022) that the university possessed an undisclosed number of Indigenous ancestral human remains. As the Office of the Provost noted in its official statement, while "some efforts have been made in the past" to repatriate "items," the process "was never completed" (Girod et al. 2022). KU thus later pledged to lead "efforts to support those impacted by the incomplete process started at the university decades ago" (Bichelmeyer et al. 2022). Again, KU administrators deploy similar moves to Syverud's: the distancing of blame; the embrace of strategic historical "forgetting"; the usage of passive voice meant to dilute KU's role as central agent of violence; and the minimization of *present* violence and trauma through the assertion that the "incomplete process" began "decades ago"—suggesting the university's commitment to Indigenous rights for "decades," even while it held the remains of nearly 400 Indigenous peoples on its very campus in 2022 (Kunze 2022).

This news deeply distressed Indigenous students, faculty, and staff on campus who represent a range of tribes with different traditions and practices of death and burial (Hodison 2022). It also soon came to light, however, that four buildings on campus housed the majority of the remains—including Lippincott Hall, the home of KU's Indigenous Studies Program. The situation clearly demonstrates the institutional paradox that Lowe explicates: The university's institutional recognition and valuing of Indigenous studies programs too often depend upon ongoing violence toward the Indigenous students, faculty, teachers, and staff who largely staff and support these programs. Moreover, as Indigenous historian Amy Lonetree (2012) emphasizes, the violent collection and storage of Indigenous human remains in educational facilities like museums maintains a nineteenth-century colonial practice that serves a foundational and "educational" function for contemporary university disciplines. Scholars like Samuel G. Morton, recognized contemporarily as "the father of physical anthropology," actively collected human remains for pseudoscientific "studies" that measured cranial capacity and skull shape to support white supremacist, imperialist theories of white, European intellectual superiority (Lonetree 2012, 12).

Ultimately, then, given KU's decades-long delay toward repatriation up until the moment of the inadvertent discovery of the Indigenous remains in 2022, one might assume that the institutional embarrassment and fear of legal repercussions associated with the 1990 Native American Graves Protection and Repatriation Act (NAGPRA) perhaps rendered the repatriation of Indigenous remains and funerary items a "priority" for administrators (Bichelmeyer et al. 2022), rather than the decades of embodied, spiritual harm that Indigenous students, faculty, and staff may have experienced while unknowingly learning and working within a building that improperly and non-consensually housed sacred, ancestral remains.[8]

In addition to overt examples like those of SU and KU, the logics of repackaging racial trauma and violence as teaching/learning opportunity intrinsically structures many dominant approaches to "social justice" pedagogy in the classroom. The recent push for critical pedagogy scholars toward cultivating "brave spaces" in the classroom showcases this version of benevolent gaslighting. These spaces utilize "ground rules" like "agree to disagree; don't take things personally; challenge by choice; respect and no attacks" (Arao and Clemens 2013, 143).

---

8 The news that KU had been housing ancestral remains improperly for so many years was deeply distressing Indigenous students such as Tweesna Rose Mills of the Shoshone-Yakama-Umatilla Nations and Myltin Bighorn of Fort Peck Sioux, for example, who publicly noted their anger and sadness as a result of this instance of Indigenous erasure (Hodison 2022). Upon learning that the remains had been stored in the same building as the Indigenous Studies Program, Mills expressed her frustration at the fact that Lippincott Hall is "one of the only places that we feel we can go to as Indigenous people because we don't have a room, we don't have a building—we have to create these spaces, and for them to literally take that way by putting unidentified Indigenous human remains there … it's like no one even cared to this day" (Hodison 2022).

   BENEVOLENT DIVERSITY

Robin DiAngelo and Özlem Sensoy (2014, 4) similarly offer "guidelines" for students for "engaging constructively with social justice content," which include practices like "striv[ing] for intellectual humility," "let[ting] go of personal anecdotal evidence and look[ing] at broader societal patterns," and "notic[ing] your own defensive reactions." Both of these perspectives not only depend upon easy, individualistic, and overly simplified divisions between emotion and logic but also suggest racial injury in the classroom as pedagogically "constructive," especially for the white students implicitly positioned as the audience for such "guidelines." Importantly, early pedagogical training in graduate school as graduate teaching associates sometimes reinforce these narratives. Writing program administrators often advise early-career instructors "to minimize their embodiment and their affect at all times" to address gendered and racialized microaggressions in the classroom by calmly helping students "reason through" flaws in their thinking (Prasad and Prasad 2023, 77). As already apparent to most multiply marginalized, racialized instructors, these moments, which some might refer to as "teachable moments," can—in reality—be deeply fraught, confusing, and even frightening. Broader pedagogical narratives that position teachers as romantic martyrs and students as inherently benevolent often further exacerbate this discomfort (Prasad 2022b). Such narratives obfuscate a recognition of the inequities and traumas that make marginalized teachers' work difficult or even impossible in the immediate present (Brewer 2020, 47) and send the message to racialized instructors that their existence lies secondary to (white) students' comfort and "learning."

References

Ahmed, Sara. 2012. *On Being Included: Racism and Diversity in Institutional Life.* Durham, NC: Duke University Press.

Anderson, Erika M., and Matt Oates. 1998. "Tracing Black History at Ohio State." *The Lantern*, August 2. https://www.thelantern.com/1998/08/tracing-black-history-at-ohio-state/.

Anderson, Greta. 2019. "History Repeats Itself." *Inside Higher Ed*, November 24. https://www.insidehighered.com/news/2019/11/25/syracuse-students -demand-change-campus-after-two-weeks-hate.

Arao, Brian, and Kristi Clemens. 2013. "From Safe Spaces to Brave Spaces: A New Way to Frame Dialogue Around Diversity and Social Justice." *The Art of Effective Facilitation: Reflections from Social Justice Educators*, edited by Lisa M. Landreman, 135–150. Sterling, VA: Stylus Publishing.

Bichelmeyer, Barbara, Nicole Hodges Persley, and Melissa Peterson. 2022. "RE: Update on the Repatriation of Native American Ancestral Remains Held by KU." Email to Pritha Prasad, September 5, 2022.

Brewer, Meaghan. 2020. *Conceptions of Literacy: Graduate Instructors and the Teaching of First-Year Composition*. Logan: Utah State University Press.

Brown, Danielle K., and Rachel R. Mourão. 2022. "No Reckoning for the Right: How Political Ideology, Protest Tolerance, and News Consumption Affect Support Black Lives Matter Protests." *Political Communication* 39 (6): 737–754.

Cherry, Myisha. 2021. *The Case for Rage: Why Anger Is Essential to Anti-Racist Struggle*. Oxford: Oxford University Press, 2021.

Cooper, Brittney C. 2016. "The Racial Politics of Time." TED Talk, February 21. https://www.ted.com/talks/brittney_cooper_the_racial_politics_of_time /transcript.

Davis, Angelique M., and Rose Ernst. 2019. "Racial Gaslighting." *Politics, Groups, and Identities* 7 (4): 761–774.

DiAngelo, Robin, and Özlem Sensoy. 2014. "Leaning In: A Student's Guide to Engaging Constructively with Social Justice Content." *Radical Pedagogy* 11 (1): 1–24.

Dong, Harvey. 2009. "Third World Liberation Comes to San Francisco State and UC Berkeley." *Chinese America: History and Perspectives*, 95–106.

Duggan, Lisa. 2012. *The Twilight of Equality?: Neoliberalism, Cultural Politics, and the Attack on Democracy*. Boston: Beacon Press.

Ferguson, Roderick A. 2012. *The Reorder of Things: The University and Its Pedagogies of Minority Difference*. Minneapolis: University of Minnesota Press.

Ferguson, Roderick A. 2017. *We Demand: The University and Student Protests*. Berkeley: University of California Press.

Flowers, Deidre B. 2005. "The Launching of the Student Sit-in Movement: The Role of Black Women at Bennett College." *Journal of African American History* 90 (1–2): 52–63.

Girod, Doug, Barbara A. Bichelmeyer, Nicole Hodges Persley, and Melissa Peterson. 2022. "RE: Statement on the Repatriation of Native American Ancestral Remains Held by KU." Email to Pritha Prasad, September 20, 2022.

Graves, Clint G., and Leland G. Spencer. 2022. "Rethinking the Rhetorical Epistemics of Gaslighting." *Communication Theory* 32 (1): 48–67.

Heitner, Devorah. 2021. "Kids Pay the Price for Adults' Failures to Act Against Racism." CNN, January 5. https://www.cnn.com/2021/01/05/opinions/nyt-groves-galligan-adults-failed-on-racism-heitner/index.html.

Herner, Hannah. 2016. "#ReclaimOSU Releases Statement Regarding Treatment at Sit-In." *The Lantern*, April 7. https://www.thelantern.com/2016/04/reclaimosu-releases-statement-regarding-treatment-at-sit-in/.

Hodison, Maya. 2022. "Native American Students Mourn After Ancestral Remains Discovered in KU's Possession." *Lawrence Times*, September 22. https://lawrencekstimes.com/2022/09/22/ku-students-mourn-ancestors/.

Kunze, Jenna. 2022. "University of Kansas Says It Has Native American Remains in Museum Collection." Native News Online, September 21. https://nativenewsonline.net/sovereignty/university-of-kansas-says-its-has-native-american-remains-in-museum-collection.

Kynard, Carmen. 2013. *Vernacular Insurrections: Race, Black Protest, and the New Century in Composition-Literacies Studies*. Albany: State University of New York Press.

Kynard, Carmen. 2018. "Stayin Woke: Race-Radical Literacies in the Makings of a Higher Education." *College Composition and Communication* 69 (3): 519–529.

Ladson-Billings, Gloria, and William F. Tate. 1995. "Toward a Critical Race Theory of Education." *Teachers College Record* 97 (1): 47–68.

Levin, Dan. 2020. "A Racial Slur, a Viral Video, and a Reckoning." *New York Times*, December 26. https://www.nytimes.com/2020/12/26/us/mimi-groves-jimmy-galligan-racial-slurs.html.

Lin, Angel, Ryuko Kubota, Su Motha, Wendy Wang, and Shelley Wong. 2006. "Theorizing Experiences of Asian Women Faculty in Second and Foreign-Language Teacher Education." *"Strangers" of the Academy: Asian Women Scholars in Higher Education*, edited by Guofang Li and Gulbahar H. Beckett, 56–84. Sterling, VA: Stylus Publishing.

Linebaugh, Riley. 2022. "Colonial Fragility: British Embarrassment and the So-Called 'Migrated Archives.'" *Journal of Imperial and Commonwealth History* 50 (4): 729–756.

Lonetree, Amy. 2012. *Decolonizing Museums: Representing Native America in National and Tribal Museums*. Chapel Hill: University of North Carolina Press.

Lowe, Lisa. 1998. "The International Within the National: American Studies and Asian American Critique." *Cultural Critique* 40: 29–47.

Maraj, Louis M. 2020. *Black or Right: Anti/Racist Campus Rhetorics*. Denver, CO: Utah State University Press.

McMahon, Julie. 2019. "Inside 10 Days That Shook Syracuse University: Fear, Power, Confusion, and 'Not Again.'" Syracuse.com, November 22. https://www.syracuse.com/syracuse-university/2019/11/inside-10-days-that-shook-syracuse-university-fear-power-confusion-and-not-again.html.

Melamed, Jodi. 2011. *Represent and Destroy: Rationalizing Violence in the New Racial Capitalism.* Minneapolis: University of Minnesota Press.

Meyerhoff, Eli. 2019. *Beyond Education: Radical Studying for Another World.* Minneapolis: University of Minnesota Press.

Miller, Michael. 2015. "Black Grad Student on Hunger Strike in Mo. after Swastika Drawn with Human Feces." *Washington Post*, November 6. https://www.washingtonpost.com/news/morningmix/wp/2015/11/06/black-grad-student-on-hunger-strike-in-mo-after-swastika-drawn-with-human-feces/.

"Ohio State Commemorates 50th Anniversary of Protests for Racial Equality." 2018. Ohio State News, May 1. https://news.osu.edu/ohio-state-commemorates-50th-anniversary-of-protests-for-racial-equality/.

Ngo, Helen. 2019. "'Get Over It'? Racialised Temporalities and Bodily Orientations in Time." *Journal of Intercultural Studies* 40 (2): 239–253.

Ore, Ersula J. 2019. *Lynching: Violence, Rhetoric, and American Identity.* Jackson: University Press of Mississippi.

Ore, Ersula J., and Matthew Houdek. 2020. "Lynching in Times of Suffocation: Toward a Spatiotemporal Politics of Breathing." *Women's Studies in Communication* 43 (4): 443–458.

Palmer, Tyrone S. 2017. "'What Feels More Than Feeling?' Theorizing the Unthinkability of Black Affect." *Critical Ethnic Studies* 3 (2): 31–56.

Prasad, Pritha. 2022a. "(Anti)Racist World-Making in the University: Reinventing Student Work." *Inventing the Discipline: Student Work in Composition Studies*, edited by Stacey Waite and Peter Wayne Moe. Anderson, SC: Parlor Press.

Prasad, Pritha. 2022b. "Backchannel Pedagogies: Unsettling Racial Teaching Moments and White Futurity." *Present Tense* 9 (2). https://www.presenttensejournal.org/volume-9/backchannel-pedagogies-unsettling-racial-teaching-moments-and-white-futurity/.

Prasad, Kriti, and Pritha Prasad. 2023. "Affective Solidarity and Trauma-Informed Possibilities: A Comparative Analysis of the Classroom and the Clinic." In *Trauma-Informed Pedagogy in Higher Education: A Faculty Guide for Teaching and Learning*, edited by Ernest Stromberg, 69–88. New York: Routledge.

Riedner, Rachel, and Kevin Mahoney. 2008. *Democracies to Come: Rhetorical Action, Neoliberalism, and Communities of Resistance.* Lanham, MD: Lexington Books.

Rojas, Fabio. 2010. *From Black Power to Black Studies: How a Radical Social Movement Became an Academic Discipline.* Baltimore: Johns Hopkins University Press.

Soldatenko, Michael. 2022. "The Bay Area Third World Strikes, 1968–1969: Coalitional Activism and Chicanx Campus Politics." *Journal of Latinos and Education* 32(2): 474–491.

Solórzano, Daniel G., and Tara J. Yosso. 2022. "Critical Race Methodology: Counter-Storytelling as an Analytical Framework for Education Research." *Qualitative Inquiry* 8 (1): 23–44.

Syverud, Kent. 2019. "Syracuse University Chancellor Kent Syverud Speaks to University Senate About Racist Incidents." Syracuse.com, November 20, https://www.youtube.com/watch?v=9OVQepF8foo.

Tarlep, Sharon, and Douglas Belkin. 2015. "Mizzou Athletic Department Backs Black Football Players on Boycott—WSJ." *Wall Street Journal*, November 8. https://www.wsj.com/articles/minority-players-on-university-of-missouri-football-team-threaten-boycott-1446997013.

Trimbur, John. 2019. "Composition's Left and the Struggle for Revolutionary Consciousness." *Writing Democracy: The Political Turn In and Beyond the Trump Era*, edited by Shannon Carter, Deborah Mutnick, Stephen Parks, and Jessica Pauszek, 27–50. New York: Routledge.

UC San Diego. 2024. "About Thurgood Marshall College." https://marshall.ucsd.edu/about-us/index.html.

Umemoto, Karen. 1989. " 'On Strike!' San Francisco State College Strike, 1968–69: The Role of Asian American Students." *Amerasia Journal* 15 (1): 3–41.

Weaver, Teri. 2019. "#NotAgainSU: A Timeline of Racist Incidents at Syracuse University." Syracuse.com, November 22. https://www.syracuse.com/syracuse-university/2019/11/notagainsu-a-timeline-of-racist-incidents-at-syracuse-university.html.

Winant, Howard. 2001. *The World Is a Ghetto Race and Democracy Since World War II*. New York: Basic Books.

Woodson, Ashley N. 2017. " 'There Ain't No White People Here': Master Narratives of the Civil Rights Movement in the Stories of Urban Youth." *Urban Education* 52 (3): 316–342.

Zimmerman, Jonathan. 2021. "When Students Stumble, Colleges Should Turn to Restorative Justice Before Expulsion." *Washington Post*, January 28. www.washingtonpost.com, https://www.washingtonpost.com/opinions/2021/01/28/when-students-stumble-colleges-should-turn-restorative-justice-before-expulsion/.

"So What Is the Lesson?"

How do we *fix* racial trauma or harm? Move beyond damned if they do or don't? Won't you help me read it some other way?

Say, did this really happen? How could we learn from what and whom we deem unreal? How 'bout you just forget how you *feel* for a bit and think for collective good?

Would it make sense to say that violence makes race? Put the impact aside and just listen, save face, extend some grace from the floor? Could we maybe defend the humanity of *everyone* for a minute? When's the time for peace and listening?

No, but how can we be *generous* in facing violence, though? You wanna just throw out everything that we've overcome? When is this cycle of brutality done? Could *you* be the brave one to teach us how to learn from this tragedy ad nauseam?

https://doi.org/10.7330/9781646428489.c003b

4 · "No, but This Actually Happened"

Receive a list of questions for an upcoming editor position interview at —— *Studies*, one a "thought experiment": Imagine reviewers deem a senior scholar of color's piece "accept with revisions"; the author agrees to proceed, but against your editorial guidance they protest on each level: no major, minor, or copy edits for this make-believe PoC—no, these racially charged recommendations and the (allegedly) racist "requirement" to explain changes can't do. Think through this scenario, respond, and tell these white interviewers how your editorial philosophy would make do.

When eventually asked in the Zoom interview, refuse to answer and instead mention the benevolent gaslight (by name, citation) of using a person of color's experience as object lesson for learning more about candidates. "No, but this actually happened," they insist. So recast an explanation that makes clear discomfort with resisting their mission to learn from some racialized other's trauma.

"No, but *the thing is*, this actually happened."

——

https://doi.org/10.7330/9781646428489.c004a

In the April 18, 2024, episode of BBC's *HARDtalk*, host Stephen Sackur sits with Guyanese President Irfan Ali, a round desk topped with white roses—each, pristine, rests in its individual glass of water, huddled—serves a centerpiece between them. "Over the next decade or two decades it is expected that there will be $150 billion worth of oil and gas extracted off your coast. It's an extraordinary figure" (*HARDtalk* 2024) Sackur, black-framed spectacles tilted down, balks, "Think of it in practical terms: that means according to many experts more than 2 billion tons of carbon emissions will come from your seabed from those reserves and be released into the atmosphere. I don't know if you as a head of state went to the COP [Conference on the Parties] in Dubai—"

"Let me stop you right there." Ali interrupts, right hand arched firm, "Let me stop you right there. Do you know that Guyana has a forest—*forever*—that is the size of England and Scotland combined?" The host barely budges, vision clamped on Ali, "A forest that stores 19.5 gigatons of carbon. A forest that *we* have kept alive. A forest that we have kept alive."

Glasses off in one hand, Sackur knives the air forward with the pointer finger of his next, "Does that give you the right, does that give you the right—"

"No no no, le— le— does that give *you*—" Ali maneuvers in counter.

"To release—" white benevolence powers through.

"Does that give *you* the right—"

"To release all this carbon?" Sackur just *manages* to ask.

—

Respectability. Grit. "Pull yourself up by your bootstraps." "What doesn't kill you makes you stronger." The American Dream. "All's well that ends well." "Turn the other cheek." Resilience. "When they go low, we go high." Learning welled in violence. When life gives you lemons . . . "You have to work twice as hard to get half as far." "Cast down your bucket where you are."

—

"DISCRIMINATION IS WRONG" claims a flyer in bold white lettering with "NO VACCINE PASSPORT" nestled against the declaration; both overlay a dated photograph captioned "Staff and students of the Methodist residential school—1880" (Siekmann 2021b). The flip side calls for an abolition to COVID-19 pandemic restrictions. Approximately 52,000 copies of the missive arrive at the homes of Vancouver-Quadra riding residents in September 2021 on behalf of People's Party of Canada candidate Renate Siekmann (Little 2021). The graphic reminds of the only-months-earlier unearthing of the remains of 215 Indigenous children in Kamloops, British Columbia, and, against ire, on Twitter, Siekmann (2021a) maintains, "This analogy may make some uncomfortable or angry but this is a hard and important conversation to have."

—

President Ali persists, "Does that give you the right to lecture us on climate change? I am going to lecture *you* on climate change" (*HARDtalk* 2024). He digs in, returning serve with selfsame right pointer, "Because we have kept this forest alive that stores 19.5 gigatons of carbon that *you* enjoy, that the world enjoy [*sic*], that you don't pay us for, that you don't value, that you don't see a value in, that the people of Guyana has kept alive. Guess what?" Center-framed, Sackur momentarily visually lost to BBC's shot, the president issues, "We have the lowest deforestation rate in the world. And guess what?" The camera defaults to neutral, the host perched attentive to countering position, "Even with our greatest exploration of the oil and gas resource we have now, we will still be, ah, net zero. Guyana will still be net zero, with all our exploration—"

"Couple of points," the BBC journalist still offers.

"—we will still be net zero."

"Pow—" with vertical palms, Sackur halves the air to reach to interrupt again.

"No no—"

"—powerful words, Mr. President."

"—no, hold, hold, hold!"

"A couple—"

"I am not completed as yet," Ali gestures the host to ease off, to stop, right palm up to frame his message defense. "I am not finished as yet. I am just not finished as yet. Because this is the hypocrisy that exists in the world." The politician moves back to attack: "We—the world in the last fifty years has lost 65 percent of all its biodiversity. We have kept our biodiversity. Are you valuing it? Are you ready to pay for it? When is the developed world going to pay for it?"

"Well—" Sackur cuts in, off-screen voice now bottom-left-margined.

"Or are you in the pockets—"

"—y-you—"

"Are you in the pockets of those who have damaged the environment?" Voice raised and pointer bouncing, Ali wields "Are you in the pockets? Are you and your system in the pockets of those who destroyed the environment through the Industrial Revolution and now lecturing us? Are you in their pockets? Are you paid by them? Are you paid to keep their message alive?"

"Alright, alright, Mr. President!"

"There is no hypocrisy in our position."

—

"Be the change you want to see in the world." Based on a true story. Make an example of yourself. "Only a fool learns from his own mistakes. The wise man learns from the mistakes of others."

—

As the last of three points highlighted in addressing media after the Ferguson Grand Jury's decision not to indict Officer Darren Wilson for the 2014 murder of Michael Brown, then-President Barrack Obama makes this appeal:

> Finally, we need to recognize that the situation in Ferguson speaks to broader challenges that we still face as a nation. The fact is, in too many parts of this country, a deep distrust exists between law enforcement and communities of color. Some of this is the result of the legacy of racial discrimination in this

country. And this is tragic, because nobody needs good policing more than poor communities with higher crime rates. The good news is we know there are things we can do to help. (Obama White House 2014)

Brown's "crime," shrugging a jaywalking warning, while "fitting the description," too, dissolves in a patronizing rhetoric where Black death moves, motivates white institutional "help." Justice means "working with law enforcement officials to make sure their ranks are representative of the communities they serve. We know that makes a difference" because state violence by Black hands wouldn't look as plain (Obama White House 2014). "It means" police trainings, intracommunity surveillance, that "good people on all sides of this debate . . . start tackling much-needed criminal justice reform" (Obama White House 2014). Don't be mad y'all, "those should be the *lessons* that we draw from these tragic events" (Obama White House 2014).

—

Ellen R. Yates self-publishes *George Floyd Legacy: Learning from Tragedy* on May 2, 2023 (Yates 2023). The children's book sketches Floyd's story as a victim of police brutality, "encourages children to think critically about how they can help create a more just and equitable society," and includes discussion questions aimed to rally engagement with racial justice efforts in the US ("George Floyd" 2023).

—

Police1.com—proclaimed "#1 resource for law enforcement online," tallying over "2 million visitors per month" ("Our Mission" 2024) —features in its "Police Training" resources: "Rapid response: Officer's mindset, tactics should have changed when George Floyd went from 'man resisting' to 'man down,'" subtitled "As this incident leads the news, it is imperative we identify lessons we can apply to training, policy and community relations," published swiftly on May 27, 2020, two days after Floyd's death (Friese 2020). A Birmingham, Alabama, report's headline three months later confirms "Police departments learning lessons from George Floyd's death." In the words of Pleasant Grove, Alabama, Lt. Daniel Reid: "We did some racial diversity training and racial profiling especially in our case, we did training across the board. Officers and dispatchers who answered calls. We did racial sensitivity training" (Collins 2020).

—

"We need to recognize that this is not just an issue for Ferguson," President Obama repeats, "this is an issue for America," as though most poor Black people—disenfranchised, made criminal, essentialized—could stake claim to some (unraced, collective) body politic (Obama White House 2014). "We have made enormous progress in race relations over the course of the past several decades. I've witnessed that in my own life. And to deny that progress I think is to deny America's capacity for change," whereas the source, that anti-Black violence funding "progress," remains the same.

—

In "Racial Bias Trainings Surged After George Floyd's Death," Candice Norwood (2021) reports that "Research indicates that simply becoming aware of a bias does not change behavior," citing studies that 1960s approaches in corporate America endure today. So "Even as diversity programs have expanded at major companies since the 1990s, conditions haven't changed significantly for underrepresented communities." So much for workshopping whiteness away; so little for making "good" use of killing us.

—

The White House press briefing continues: "But what is also true is that there are still problems and communities of color aren't just making these problems up. Separating that from this particular decision, there are issues in which the law too often feels as if it is being applied in discriminatory fashion" (Obama White House 2014). How exactly could one isolate a most immediate example, an instance so blatant and legible, from its pattern? How to talk of the law *feeling* one way or the other while caging so large a percentage of Black America?

"I don't think that's the norm," the exception overrepresents: "I don't think that's true for the majority of communities or the vast majority of law enforcement officials. But these are real issues. And we have to lift them up and not deny them or try to tamp them down." Diplomacy's pendulum oscillates unbound:

> What we need to do is to understand them and figure out how do we make more progress. And that can be done. That won't be done by throwing bottles. That won't be done by smashing car windows. That won't be done by using this as an excuse to vandalize property. And it certainly won't be done by hurting anybody. So, to those in Ferguson, there are ways of channeling your concerns constructively and there are ways of channeling your concerns destructively. (Obama White House 2014)

Construct narratives from the dead, bred for the white nation they already built. Guilt them criminal in terms immanent to their imminent destruction.

—

The Guardian Nigeria columnist Aladesohun Sola (2020), in "Lessons from George Floyd Unintentional Killing," takes "moral lessons" from the tragedy that Floyd's alleged tender of counterfeit currency raises "questioning eyebrows at his character," citing Plato to deem Floyd somehow unhappy. According to Sola, "His being stiff-necked made Derek Chauvin pin his neck"; Floyd's story neatly aligns with how, across the US, "it is stories of Blacks' aggression, crime and violence that one hears. Coke, weed, crack. etc." Floyd should have gone to the station with officers, Sola preaches. His death, nevertheless, teaches us "how delicate the human's life is," how protestors aided the spread of COVID-19, how much of a "law-abiding citizen" Chauvin represents (Sola 2020).

—

"Michael Brown's parents understand what it means to be constructive" —their response to trauma easy fodder, the perfect example to keep law, affect, "progress" in order (Obama White House 2014). "The vast majority of peaceful protesters, they understand it as well. Those of you who are watching tonight understand that there's never an excuse for violence, particularly when there are a lot of people in goodwill out there who are willing to work on these issues." And so even the audience somewhere out there obediently consuming the White House presser knows how to take directive, how to heed the inherent *good* of learning patience from anti-Black murder.

"On the other hand, those who are only interested in focusing on the violence and just want the problem to go away need to recognize that we do have work to do here, and we shouldn't try to paper it over. Whenever we do that, the anger may momentarily subside, but over time it builds up and America isn't everything that it could be." Shame on you for stopping the empire from using tragedy to grow, for illuming the care for infrastructure and property and the "normal function of society" over victims of unnecessary murder! How dare you! "And I am confident that if we focus our attention on the problem and we look at what has happened in communities around the country effectively, then we can make *progress* not just in Ferguson, but in a lot of other cities and communities around the country. Okay?"

—

Black death made "opportunity"—from multiple origins, Old French *opportunité*, Latin *opportūnitās* signaling "favorable circumstance(s)" (*Oxford English Dictionary* 2023)—alas.

—

In response to a query from the press on a possible trip to Ferguson, President Obama shares that US Attorney General Eric Holder and a Justice Department team visited there: "They have done some very good work. As I said, the vast majority of the community has been working very hard to try to make sure that this becomes an opportunity for us to seize the moment and turn this into a positive situation" (Obama White House 2014).

Rinse. Repeat. Three years to the week of Floyd's death, ABC News (2023) runs an interview with Minnesota Attorney General Keith Ellison on his release of *Break the Wheel: Ending the Cycle of Police Violence*. The book seeks to unpack, from the perspective of the lead prosecutor in the Chauvin case, how those proceedings "[offer] insights for future cases of police brutality, aiming to foster justice, accountability and the end of the violent cycle within the criminal justice system." Rinse. Repeat.

—

"But I think that we have to make sure that we focus at least as much attention on all those positive activities that are taking place as we do on a handful of folks who end up using this as an excuse to misbehave or to break the law or to engage in violence" (Obama White House 2014), as the law, in literal effect, flakes in favor of state apparatuses in its anti-Black extraction. "I think that it's going to be very important," *in loco parentis* the admonition proceeds, "and I think the media is going to have a responsibility as well to make sure that we focus on Michael Brown's parents, and the clergy, and the community leaders, and the civil rights leaders, and the activists, and law enforcement officials who have been working very hard to try to find better solutions—long-term solutions—to this issue."

—

"After George Floyd's Death, a Time to Listen and Learn," suggests the *Los Angeles Times* (Lelyveld 2020). *Harper's Bazaar*, meanwhile, asks, "What Have We Learnt from the Murder of George Floyd?" (E. Alexander 2021). NPR instead offers "10 Questions About Empathy in America, a Year After George Floyd's Death" (Chappell 2021).

—

"There is inevitably going to be some negative reaction, and it will make for good TV" (Obama White House 2014)—Black(ened) rage but entertainment. "But what we want to do is to make sure that we're also focusing on those who can offer the kind of real progress that we know is possible, that the vast majority of people in Ferguson, the St. Louis region, in Missouri, and around the country are looking for." What *good*, really, could injustice do but inspire universal learning?

——

On their page "Lessons Learned One Year After the Murder of George Floyd," nonprofit organization Big Brothers Big Sisters of America affirms its commitment to "all people of diverse backgrounds" through its engagement in "inclusive and actionable" work (Big Brothers Big Sisters of America 2021). After examples, a grayscale photo of a young white man locked in a shared smile with a Black boy beckons readers to "INVEST IN A CHILD'S FUTURE." Suffer little children that ye might not cause to spur but be yet saved by such benevolence.

——

President Obama resolves, arced rightward to his audience, ends, "And I want to be partners with those folks. And we need to lift up that kind of constructive dialogue that's taking place. All right" (Obama White House 2014).

——

"Faith"-inspired disability activist Amy Julia Becker (2021) writes on her website, in "3 Things I've Learned One Year After George Floyd's Death," that "1. Black Lives Matter to white people," that suddenly we live "in a new moment of white people committing to support Black people in their demands for justice"; that "2. Police cultures can change"—no need to abolish or defund them; that "3. Everyone can respond with loving action to the harm and injustice of racism": some can even buy Chromebooks for poor kids during the pandemic and jolt conversations within their church about historical racism within them, as though said "white American church" could ever divorce itself from genociding Natives, enslaving Blacks in this collective moment of *giving-back*. And though Becker claims that "George Floyd should not have died, nor should many men and women before him," what of the people who stay dying onward, after, now that white benevolence temporally buries Black state violence with goodly white deference?

   "NO, BUT THIS ACTUALLY HAPPENED"

On Netflix's popular and critically acclaimed *You*, protagonist Joe, average white male serial killer, obsesses narratively, typically through white women objects. Slow as he goes, that second-person ma(r)king offers viewers their stories through his frame—that *oh so deep* love that controls, that gives anything ever in its name, until it all ends in murder. *You* wants that you see from a tame, slow-burn violence where an object of affection unpacks for you the inherent good in it, persisted, of course, from his narrative, "humanizing" perspective.

—

When one "you" becomes Love, literally by name, she—*You* reveals—this white woman object emerges a serial killer too. They marry.

In season 3, episode 2, as the two prepare to bury one of their victims, Love cries, "You act all pure and noble like you have reasons for what you do and when you do it. But when I do, I'm crazy, right?! Like I'm some manic nutjob"—her white feminist ethic binarizing the violence of gender (Tree 2021a).

—

"I'm a not a violent person," Joe proposes, disheveled. "What if sometimes you are? What if that's normal?" the couples' therapist rejoins. As each murder flashes back through Joe's mind, "I don't wanna hurt *anyone*," emphasis accented with raised eyebrows. "I believe you," the therapist soothes him.

—

A rare racialized mention, that season's third episode, "Missing White Woman Syndrome," probes a post–George Floyd attention: "Missing White Woman Syndrome is America's favorite pastime next to porn," chimes the Black-woman librarian (Scott 2021a). Joe, befuddled by his coworker's claim, has their blind white colleague Dante explain. But with its power dynamics lost on him, momentarily frustrated, she further elaborates on the message sent: "White ladies deserve to be rescued. The rest of us can fend for ourselves."

Later, in episode 4, in pitching to that librarian, Marienne, that her assumption that he grew up rich was wrong, in unpacking his relationship with books: "We straddled the poverty line my entire childhood and I *escaped* with books. I learned all about them like you wanna know everything about that one beautiful thing. It saves your miserable life" (Scott 2021b). Those things, turned objects of desire makes this whiteman serial killer a victim who could only come whole again controlling and remaking them—this Joe "restores" old books. "So I misjudged a little, maybe." With a snarky comment, he elicits an apology. "And I guess I might have to like you after all."

Our narrator, by episode 5, slips, trips, into old habits, refers to this Black-woman library director as "you," but just once (Tree 2021b). He *wills* to fight it. But later, while stalking from his car, his didactic frame maintains that this time is different. "I can't completely cage what's inside of me, or when it bursts out it comes for blood," he shares, in the instruction-manual tone of a pedantic giver. "Better to feed it just enough to keep it in check. Keep it on a leash, take it out for walks, make sure *it* knows the rules." He offers a list of guidelines for moving *forward*. "So now I have *you*, Marienne . . . I've felt more alive in these last few days watching you than I've felt in a long, long time, Marienne." He commits to juggling "the two of you" carefully. "Things will be different this time." Indeed, things will.

—

"W.O.M.B," episode 6, finds the narrator rifling through Marienne's home to assert freely, "You take care of books and art and young minds; who takes care of you?" as he fixes a leaky faucet (Tree 2021c). But he changes his mind, equivocates, and decides on reintroducing the drip, "No. No, no, no. This is not why I'm here. I'm here, well, to figure out why I'm here. Why you, Marienne?" He admits that he likes following "you . . . and that inner part of me that needs, uh, *this* is mostly satiated, but in the spirit of self-awareness and maybe conquering that inner *thing*"—because this violence inside (which the previous episode warns is an animal) triangulates through those made his things in pursuit—"I ask again, why am I drawn to you?"

While hiding under her bed, he next frames the intrusion as means, as "all to prove *you* aren't worth it. You are just a fleeting crush," disposable.

And when at home, with his wife and child, on taking a bite of some freshly baked good, the narrator divulges in his object's absence, steers "Let me be clear. You fascinate me. But Love is my soulmate, mother of my child, love of my life. And my job as a father and husband is to keep it that way."

Our narrator then rummages your work office and finds documents pertaining to addiction recovery, charges against you for child endangerment, neglect, abuse, the bad-Black-mother trope rearing its ugly head—at first "this can't be right." Then "Then, the more I know, the less I understand. Who are you? What I do know? Your problems are serious. You're a mess." So, citing his stable family life—such a black and white difference, daggers palpable—he "can't have anything to do with your planet of red flags. The itch has been scratched."

—

But an altercation between you and your ex-husband leads to the narrator being chastised for the compulsion to "run up here like some white knight," and as he flashes back through his history of objects of obsession, hurling insults: "I see it now." This is why "you. You're a pattern." The Black woman made thing, a code-breaking hack for diagnosis. "You're a lost lamb attracted to wolves. Ergo what I feel . . ." Your diegesis, your angry words, buried in his teach-learning. ". . . it's not because *you're special*, it's—Wait for it. It's mother issues! How's that for self-awareness?" He smiles contently in her anger's face. When you check if you're some kind of amusement, he assures you, "No, no, no. No. I'm sorry. Also, I'm not sorry. I'm not one to let bullies bully. I would've done that for anybody," that benevolence universal teaching whiteness how to better itself.

—

When you call our narrator late at night, an emergency, we meet at the sprinkler-soaked library, where, in distress over soaked books, he references African American poet/writer Jericho Brown having "discovered" your penchant for his literature earlier, trespassing. The connection leads you to reveal your past in the foster system, a similarity you intuit you share with the narrator, who, like you, longed for a mother to return to rescue, but the circumstance motivates you to be a "better mom." "I held on to that same hope," he nods, "for years. And got my ass kicked regularly for it. I think it kept me going." Violence, that great motivator. What doesn't kill you makes you stronger. Next, you offer the injustice your white ex-husband (local celeb newscaster) has dealt in shared substance abuse, constructing a tropic (anti-Black) narrative through "manipulating the system" and of course, "I think we can both agree white men get a million chances in life," so, believable, he maintains sole custody of your child: ". . . everyone takes his word over mine because . . . who am I?"

And here he comes, that white knight, "somebody should stop him." Our narrator interjects, "I volunteer, happily." When you reveal a Parisian escape fantasy, that voice calls it a subjunctive tragedy to lose you like that, teaches us (audience) that the mistake here—in comparison to his mother—"reduced you to my issues . . . You're just who you are. You don't hide or embellish, you own your mistakes and stand up to the strikes against you"—you, a strong Black woman. Another perfectly coincidental malfunctioning sprinkler prompts the two to make out: "Oh shit. Love is gonna kill you"—murder somehow making that goodness "love" metonymic, subsumed under white obsession/possession.

—

With resignation letter in hand, the narrator enters the library, "I know now, Marienne. I know why 'you,' and it's no pattern. But today starts the next phase of my growth to know you exist, to see you, to love you even, and to never have you. Because as long as I love you, you'll be in danger." The ever-so-giving white conscience could only save this Black-woman lover by learning, by teaching, to save itself. But you admit to feelings; they're bad—children at stake. The two kiss. "I came here to quit," he says, "I thought it was gonna make this easier." But you insist "you don't have to do that." On leaving, our narrator commits: "I'll never let anyone hurt you," because your arc, your storyline, belongs to him and he will do as he will(s) to protect you—*property*.

—

As this narrator dreams of a bricolage family, you find out your ex's Channel Three intends to make a sizable donation to the library at its upcoming fundraiser—he will present the check (Chatmon 2021a). In his ploy, upset that you're reopening custody, he wants to hurt you any way, any where, even at work: "He feels ownership over me, okay? Sick as it is. And you stood up to him." This means this forbidden relationship can't happen, with your daughter's care in play. Our narrator concedes, yes, this ex represents a problem but assures (himself) that "I'll find a way to solve this one, for you."

—

When the stalking of said ex begins, the narrator accuses him of having "gaslit his way to full custody," yet eventually plants drugs in his protein shakes, replaces alarm batteries with dying ones to distort his sense of time, literally creates conditions in which someone might lose conscious grip on reality.

This ex, though, finds out the two spent time together and you, again, attempt to communicate the relationship's end—for your daughter, your recovery, you need integrity to drive intimacy. Our narrator repeats your desires verbatim, contends "Aboveboard and honest. How do I give that to you?"

—

In "Swing and a Miss," episode 8, your ex comes to pick up your daughter at the library, and the strain of her "already?," the goodbye, inspires the narrator—just scolded moments prior for taking care of your missed deadline on your behalf without asking—to "wish I could fix it. I wanna fix everything for you" (Chatmon 2021b). *To fix*, verb, originating from Latin *fixus*, past of *figĕre*, to fasten (like/as an object in place) (*Oxford English Dictionary* 2024).

And this becomes the case when, next, the night before the custody hearing, explicit photos of you get sent to your contacts and hero Joe, on the phone, offers help "if and only if you ask me to, of course," so you invite him over but he can't: "No, you've actually—You've done enough" (Chatmon 2021b).

—

But you're the one, made replaceable Black object of fancy, who does more (than you even know) as that night's adventure of sexual swinging puts his wife's Black suburbanite bestie (and her white husband) in his marriage bed, prompting visions of you and him together that head off his delayed arousal. When our narrator closes his eyes, imagines touching you and vice versa, it triggers his white partner, that capital "L" Love, to ruin the whole thing because she knows now it's not her he's fantasizing after. In the ensuing argument she loudly discloses a crime, a murder, and now, overhearing, the threatened swingers physically fight for their lives; he hunts one down motivated by the thought of not losing you, *thing he'd kill for*. And as the pair hide limp bodies of their still captors, get off on the adrenaline high of it, our narrator admits of him and his spouse "our love language is violence."

—

When the judge—who, you notice, is palling with your ex after the hearing—rules against you, our narrator tracks you to a liquor store's curb and, to assuage your crisis, reveals that he's killed someone: a man who would hurt his mother (S. Alexander 2021). Our narrator offers the revelation, the vulnerable secret-spilling, somehow to assure that you will figure the situation out: "That's what people like us do." After a kiss, he commits to relenting his marriage "I would do anything for you. It's just, ask. Just ask me"—maybe that way, from that bent, it seems like *your* idea, that *you* consented to his obsession.

You take him home, and as you two finally make love he narrates, "*This*. This is real," as if an appeal to convince his audience of the payoff, the dividend, the equity built from his violence: "I don't have to pretend

 "NO, BUT THIS ACTUALLY HAPPENED"

with you. I'm the real me." So deep runs our narrator's investment that he claims: "I'll find a way to fix everything, so that this is our every day."

With the immediacy of possible catastrophe tamed, you pledge again to not give up on your daughter, to move to New Jersey where her father plans to take her for his new hotshot cable-news job. "I'm going to lose you," the narrator upended, panics, "how can I stop this from being the end for us?" Focused, *fixated*, he resolves to kill your ex.

—

Bloodied, he returns home with our narrator asserting steadfastly, "You'll never believe that he's dead . . . because he taught you that you don't deserve a second chance, but you do. We both do." He tells himself that this is *just* chance number two, graciously teaching better than your lover prior. Surveying the tart contrast of red on his white shirt, "I don't feel bad about this . . . real evil has to be dealt with," our generous dictator commands the floor "and you don't do that by letting it live to take good people down."

—

As episode 10, "What Is Love?," begins, you call him, frazzled, with news of your ex's demise (Tree 2021d). Terrified, you say that cops questioned; none of his attempts to pacify help; you highlight your "very long history of being fucked by the system. A system that was made by and for" this ex, white men. "Can I respectfully disagree?" He chimes, then, "Not about the system but just about this moment," because it's possible to step outside of Blackness criminalized by default. "Listen, the man who hurt you, who wanted to steal your child . . . he is now gone forever"—this happenstance, murder, comes bearing gifts. *Who better to teach you how so than the one responsible for it?* He's not saying to celebrate, shit, don't "send the mugger flowers" but "This is your life getting easier." *Progress.* No judgment, you plead, before disclosing you're glad he's dead. On the phone's other end our hero smiles, lies, and says he and his wife agreed to officially separate last night. "We're both gonna be free . . . very soon." He advises you to skip town while the drama dies down, and "come with us" you suggest, daydreaming aloud about a new family built on the ruins of two. "I love you . . . I love you, and . . . Yeah, so that." He agrees to leave (with a few loose ends eventually tied) and in your excited "I can't believe we're actually doing this," he gleams: "I can. It's fate"—one insidiously constructed march toward teaching what love is.

"You invited *me*. We have a future," our narrator declares, his joy giving agency to his object (consent) finally ensnared.

—

But his wife, Love, pieces the narrative of your affair together, drugs him, and uses his phone to invite you over to their home. When you arrive, she inquires "why my husband?" twice, and then provides her own answer: "Was he kind to you? Effortlessly *get* you? . . ." You confirm, but qualify with "Something in me knew that it was too good to be true, but I just . . . he convinced me. *I* let him convince me . . ." Temporarily physically paralyzed by Love's poisoned meal, wincing from the ground of the room adjacent, our narrator interjects, "No, don't throw yourself under the bus. She's distorting things"—a desperate cling from a serial contortionist making objects/violence out of desire, of others. She goes on to reveal that he killed your ex, and you, stunned, ask, "Why would—"

"To protect you," this narrator appeals.

"Because he's obsessed with you," Love rebuts, but he insists, re-historicizing: "No, I saved you. I did a *good* thing."

After advising you to run—you become the exception, the one who "survives" his obsession, for now—sharpening the butcher-knife blade for his slaughter, Love reflects, "I mean, you gaslit me so fucking hard. I started to question . . . every single thing about myself." She walks over, readied, assured, "I'm not the problem"—the white woman scorned.

—

In their 2022 article, "African Studies Keyword: Autoethnography," published in the *African Studies Review*, two American white-women "Africanists" call on that field to "decolonize" its research purviews by

   "NO, BUT THIS ACTUALLY HAPPENED"

considering autoethnography as approach. Postdoctoral fellow Kathryn Mara and Katrina Daly Thompson, Evjue-Bascom Professor of the Humanities, both at the University of Wisconsin–Madison, harp on sustained celebrations of "objectivity" that eschew the decolonial embrace of critical self-reflexivity in African studies. While, according to the two, a nascent body of autoethnographic work exists within the field, addressing its institutions' "colonially entrenched history," nothing could appear "more urgent . . . than to address and 'right' our wrongs and to propose new, more justice-oriented research methodologies moving forward. Autoethnography is one such methodology" (Mara and Daly Thompson 2022, 389).

To introduce their stance—their "positionality"—Daly Thompson shares that in research training in Zimbabwe, later Tanzania, she married a Zanzibari man and converted to Islam. When collecting data on "Swahili women about their private lives and recording the intimate advice they gave to new brides," they came to two epiphanies: Their "near-insider perspective" and how mining, exposing, their "own private matters" seemed "only fair" (375). Never mind the extractive thrust with which they openly steal from the racial, cultural other. Colonial relations could only *get better* by centering a white woman's good virtue as cover for exploitation. Daly Thompson then concurrently merges this inspiration with their creation of a "graduate methods course on literary ethnography" that offers creative approaches for an audience mostly "from Africa."

Enter Kathryn—an assumed outsider given the "majority" African graduate student body in this department—an Anglo-American woman inspired by Daly Thompson and their course. Mara's interest in non-normative methods had survived training for her master's degree, when her proposed "creative nonfiction thesis about [her] experience as a student of European descent in a Black Studies program" prompted discouragement, disapproval from that department's chair—"too 'unconventional,'" the story goes. So Kathryn chose not to propose "an autoethnographic dissertation for fear that others would not take it as seriously as a more traditional one." In spite of these supposed marginalizations, in coauthor Katrina's course, she "finally found a space to talk about being an *umuzungu* (westerner) in Africana Studies" (375–376).

These two will deliver the necessary decolonial verve against detached objectivity in the study of Africa. They will emerge from their "positions" in white America to teach how to "decolonize" thinking on the continent—no need to consider the violence making their do-good labor possible.

In an open letter, seven self-identified African scholars in their field call for the retraction of the Mara and Daly Thompson article and an explanation from the journal's editorial team, citing "extractive methodologies" framed as "autoethnography," "poor editorial oversight[,] and [a] double standard that privileges Northern scholars' reflexivity while undermining Africans as lacking objectivity" (Mohammed et al. 2022). Despite the uproar, the long histories overshadowing these scholars' actions, nothing changes.

—

"Last summer, I disguised myself as a Black man," white Canadian journalist Sam Forster (2024a) relates on social media, "and traveled throughout the United States to document how racism persists in American society." He self-publishes his book, *Seven Shoulders: Taxonomizing Racism in Modern America* in May 2024, about his experiences the year prior, thumbing rides across the US geared in blackface. According to news reports, Forster donned an Afro wig, sported dark eye contacts, and painted his face with Maybelline mocha (Wise 2024), while he admits on X, "Writing *Seven Shoulders* was one of the hardest things I've ever done as a journalist" (Forster 2024a).

In an interview with CBC News he highlights that though he understands the distinction between his experiment and living while Black, he still agrees with his online sales pitch that hails *Seven Shoulders* as "the most important book on American race relations that has ever been written" (quoted in Maimann 2024).

Forster concludes his critical look by teaching us, graciously, about "shoulder racism" (quoted in Maimann 2024). See: "Most of what's left of racism in this country are the few, socially narrow opportunities for soft interpersonal racism." The self-appointed white race expert, as those before him, speaks with alacrity, with clear-headed universal authority: "Institutional racism (the anti-Black variety) is effectively dead."

Rest in peace, gone forever.

Those left to tend its injuries "post-racialism," in unhinged disbelief, can only plead "No, but this actually happened."

References

ABC News. 2023. "George Floyd's Death Offers Lessons on How to Stop Cycle of Police Violence: AG." Yahoo! News, May 24. https://www.yahoo.com/news /george-floyds-death-offers-lessons-195200986.html.

Alexander, Ella. 2021. "What Have We Learnt from the Murder of George Floyd?" *Harper's Bazaar.* https://www.harpersbazaar.com/uk/culture/ a36519086/george-floyd-a-year-on-opal-tometi/.

Alexander, Sasha. 2021. *You.* Season 3, episode 9, "Red Flag." Directed by Sasha Alexander, written by Michael Foley and Hillary Benefiel. Aired October 15, 2021. https://www.netflix.com/watch/81478061.

Becker, Amy Julia. 2021. "3 Things I've Learned One Year After George Floyd's Death." AmyJuliaBecker.com, May 25. https://amyjuliabecker.com/3-things -ive-learned-one-year-after-george-floyds-death/.

Big Brothers Big Sisters of America. 2021. "Lessons Learned One Year After the Murder of George Floyd." Big Brothers Big Sisters of America, May 25. https:// www.bbbs.org/2021/05/lessons-learned-one-year-after-the-murder-of -george-floyd/.

Chappell, Bill. 2021. "10 Questions About Empathy in America, a Year After George Floyd's Death." NPR, May 25. https://www.npr.org/2021/05/25 /999791624/what-george-floyds-death-has-done-for-americans-ability-to -feel-empathy.

Chatmon, Peter. 2021a. *You.* Season 3, episode 7, "We're All Mad Here." Directed by Peter Chatmon, written by Justin W. Lo and Amanda Johnson-Zetterström. Aired October 15, 2021. https://www.netflix.com/watch /81478061.

Chatmon, Peter. 2021b. *You.* Season 3, episode 8, "Swing and a Miss." Directed by Peter Chatmon, written by AB Chao and Dylan Cohen. Aired October 15, 2021. https://www.netflix.com/watch/81478061.

Collins, Alan. 2020. "Police Departments Learning Lessons from George Floyd's Death." WBRC Fox 6 News, September 1. https://www.wbrc.com/2020/09/01 /police-departments-learning-lessons-george-floyds-death/

Forster, Sam (@ForsterSam). 2024a. "Last summer, I disguised myself as a Black man and traveled throughout the United States to document how racism persists in American society." Twitter (X), May 28. https://x.com/ForsterSam /status/1795492082636795958.

Forster, Sam. 2024b. *Seven Shoulders: Taxonomizing Racism in Modern America*. Self-published.

Friese, Greg. 2020. "Rapid Response: Officer's Mindset, Tactics Should Have Changed When George Floyd Went From 'Man Resisting' to 'Man Down.'" Police1.com, May 27. https://www.police1.com/police-training/articles/rapid -response-officers-mindset-tactics-should-have-changed-when-george-floyd -went-from-man-resisting-to-man-down-Sve6Ac1Euqxd4HTM/.

George Floyd Legacy: Learning from Tragedy. 2023. Amazon.com, May 2. https:// www.amazon.ca/George-Floyd-Legacy-Learning-Tragedy/dp/B0C2ST614P.

HARDtalk. 2024. "Guyana's President: 'I Am Going to Lecture You on Climate Change.'" BBC News, April 18. https://www.bbc.co.uk/programmes /pohrnsss.

Lelyveld, Nita. 2020. "After George Floyd's Death, a Time to Listen and Learn." *Los Angeles Times*, June 6. https://www.latimes.com/california/story/2020-06 -06/george-floyd-amy-cooper-protests-voices.

Little, Simon. 2021. "B.C. PPC Candidate Slammed over Flyer Comparing Vaccine Passports to Residential Schools." Global News, September 15. https:// globalnews.ca/news/8194599/ppc-residential-school-flyer/.

Maimann, Kevin. 2024. "Black Scholars Criticize White Writer's 'Dehumanizing' Use of Blackface to Write Book on U.S. Race Relations." CBC News, June 2. https://www.cbc.ca/news/entertainment/canadian-writer-blackface -racism-1.7221168.

Mara, Kathryn, and Katrina Daly Thompson. 2022. "African Studies Keyword: Autoethnography." *African Studies Review* 65 (2): 372–398.

Mohammed, Wunpini, Chisomo Kalinga, K. Rene Odanga, Ruby Zelzer, Chris Olaoluwa Ogunmodede, Furaha Asani, and Ruth Ngozika Agbakoba. 2022. "Open Letter to African Studies Review Journal Editorial Board: Call for Retraction of Article 'African Studies Keyword: Autoethnography.'" Google Form, May 23. https://docs.google.com/forms/d/e /1FAIpQLSdKo9OgNuUoDcYMBRbuTvv2wu-sJE3StYIIaFuclGJiDevx8g /viewform.

Norwood, Candice. 2021. "Racial Bias Trainings Surged After George Floyd's Death. A Year Later, Experts Are Still Waiting for 'Bold' Change." PBS, May 25. https://www.pbs.org/newshour/nation/racial-bias-trainings-surged-after -george-floyds-death-a-year-later-experts-are-still-waiting-for-bold-change.

Obama White House. 2014. "President Obama Issues a Statement on the Ferguson Grand Jury Decision." YouTube, November 14. https://www.youtube.com /watch?v=O2BBAfWucaE&t=177s.

Oxford English Dictionary. 2024. "fix (v.), Etymology." March. https://doi.org/10.1093/OED/5007276921.

Oxford English Dictionary. 2023. "opportunity (n.), Etymology." September. https://doi.org/10.1093/OED/8163037679.

"Our Mission." 2024. police1.com. https://www.police1.com/our-mission.

Scott, John. 2021a. *You*. Season 3, episode 3, "Missing White Woman Syndrome." Directed by John Scott, written by Kara Lee Corthron and Justin W. Lo. Aired October 15, 2021. https://www.netflix.com/watch/81478061.

Scott, John. 2021b. *You*. Season 3, episode 4, "Hands Across Madre Linda." Directed by John Scott, written by Hillary Benefiel and Michael Foley. Aired October 15, 2021. https://www.netflix.com/watch/81478061.

Siekmann, Renate (@renate_siekmann). 2021a. "This analogy may make some uncomfortable or angry but this is a hard and important conversation to have." Twitter (X), September 15 (tweet deleted).

Siekmann, Renate. 2021b. "DISCRIMINATION IS WRONG." Self-published.

Sola, Aladesohun. 2020. "Lessons from George Floyd Unintentional Killing." *The Guardian Nigeria*, July 14. https://guardian.ng/opinion/lessons-from-george-floyd-unintentional-killing/.

Tree, Silver. 2021a. *You*. Season 3, episode 2, "So I Married an Axe Murderer." Directed by Silver Tree, written by Neil Reynolds and Kelli Breslin. Aired October 15, 2021. https://www.netflix.com/watch/81478061.

Tree, Silver. 2021b. *You*. Season 3, episode 5, "Into the Woods." Directed by Silver Tree, written by Mairin Reed and Amanda Johnson-Zetterström. Aired October 15, 2021. https://www.netflix.com/watch/81478061.

Tree, Silver. 2021c. *You*. Season 3, episode 6, "W.O.M.B." Directed by Silver Tree, written by Kelli Breslin and Kara Lee Corthron. Aired October 15, 2021. https://www.netflix.com/watch/81478061.

Tree, Silver, Director. 2021d. *You*. Season 3, episode 10, "What Is Love?" Directed by Silver Tree, written by Sera Gamble and Neil Reynolds. Aired October 15, 2021. https://www.netflix.com/watch/81478061.

Wise, Alana. 2024. "With Maybelline Mocha and an Afro Wig, White Author Explores 'Blackness' in a New Book." NPR, June 7. https://www.npr.org/2024/06/07/nx-s1-4984973/sam-forster-author-black-disguise-seven-shoulders.

Yates, Ellen R. 2023. *George Floyd Legacy: Learning from Tragedy*. Self-published.

"So What Is the Lesson?"

How do we *fix* racial trauma or harm? Move beyond damned if they do or don't? Won't you help me read it some other way?

Say, did this really happen? How could we learn from what and whom we deem unreal? How 'bout you just forget how you *feel* for a bit and think for collective good?

Would it make sense to say that violence makes race? Put the impact aside and just listen, save face, extend some grace from the floor? Could we maybe defend the humanity of *everyone* for a minute? When's the time for peace and listening?

No, but how can we be *generous* in facing violence, though? You wanna just throw out everything that we've overcome? When is this cycle of brutality done? Could *you* be the brave one to teach us how to learn from this tragedy ad nauseam?

https://doi.org/10.7330/9781646428489.c004b

Acknowledgments

For everything, always, I eternally thank you, Mummy, Carolin Gemma Maraj. How cruel to be forced from sitting with the sadness of losing you. May you continue to rest in peace. I could live every day for the rest of time with you, Alexis Renea McGee: I, only, see your sacrifice; words could never appreciate how you help mend the heartache that this project drew and draws. Maurice Louis McGee-Maraj, Dada forever loves you. Welcome to the world, Myers Ley McGee-Maraj—Dada forever loves you too.

Miss Sandy, I miss you and regret that this project did not give me space to mourn your passing.

Thank you, Daddy, Alfred "Freddie" Maraj. I'm grateful for the support of siblings Leiselle Donald, Lemuel "Lermie" Maraj, Laverne Maraj, and Luanna Harman. Shout-out to in-laws, Reanaldo Donald, Tammy Myers, Cyrena McGee, Sara Ramroop, and nephews and nieces, Joey, Josh, Isaiah, Dayo, Shelby, Lara, and Anthony. I continue to appreciate my extended family, especially: Merlyn Taitt, Roslyn DeLabastide, Calvin DeLabastide, Anissa Fulchan, Anson Taitt, Nadya

Murray, Clint DeLabastide, and the many on Daddy's side. May you continue your walk with God, Rita DeLabastide, Jacqueline DeLabastide, and Andre Taitt.

My ride or die group chat homies, Charles Athanasopoulos and Corinne Sugino: appreciate y'all. For kind, understanding friends like Norman Rasmussen, Sean Kamperman, Stephen Dadugblor, and my one Jamaican friend, Treviene Harris, I am grateful.

To those who have mentored, officially or unofficially, especially R. A. Judy, Carmen Kynard, Beverly Moss, Andrea Lunsford, and Wendy S. Hesford, unending thanks. Coauthors, graduate students, and mentees throughout the years, I appreciate each of you for how you have shaped my thinking. I recognize the support of colleagues like Jaclyn Rea and Kimberly Richards.

I acknowledge the direct material support of the University Press of Colorado's MMU Scholar Mini-Grants program. I thank the anonymous peer reviewers of this project for their feedback and University Press of Colorado / Utah State University Press staff and leadership for their work on this project. I'm especially appreciative of former editor Rachael Levay's steadfast commitment to its fidelity. The introduction to *The Benevolent Gaslight* is partially based on the coauthored article by Pritha Prasad and Louis M. Maraj, "I Am Not Your Teaching Moment: The Benevolent Gaslight and Epistemic Violence," *College Composition and Communication* 74.2 (2022): 322–351. I'm grateful to the readers of that piece along with others who have generously engaged the theories inherent in this book in their development at conferences, in workshops, and through small talk. To those who attempt(ed) to censor this project and any other work I do, I hope you each find whatever love you are missing in your lives.

Thanks a million, and take good care,
Lou

My parents, Arti and Sudhakar Prasad, and my sister, Kriti Prasad (Babo): I love you. Thank you—not just for the unwavering love, support, and critical realness, but also for the unseen, unquantifiable work you continue to do to sustain me. Babo, a special thanks to you. No one rides for me like you do. Tyler Hardin, my life partner and love of my life, you love me more than I deserve. I have never met anyone quite like you. Thank you for hearing me, for making me feel safe during the deep uncertainty that bookended this project, for spiraling with me just to make me feel less alone. And finally, Tesla, my perfect cat: Thank you for sitting on me at every stage of thinking and writing over the last decade I have known you. I am lucky you chose me as your home.

Thank you to my best friends for the love you have invested in me. Catherine Killough, the kind of friend who understands you so well that they will, with deep conviction, go down any path with you, even when it leads to a dead end. Zach Harvat, my co-conspirator, fellow main character, and screenname-sharing friend, thank you for your unconditional encouragement. Drew Sweet, you always know when to remind me it's not that deep. I need that. Caitlyn McLoughlin, my fake Australian friend from LA: far away in distance, but always close in heart. Colleen Morrissey, forever mom, horror queen: Being able to see and work with you every day has been such a gift. Sean Kamperman, for everything you have done to support and affirm me as both a colleague and dear friend, I am deeply grateful. And, finally, I recognize my best friends in Lawrence who continue to give me life beyond the academy. My starry ladies, Jena Dick, Lauren Dick, Blair Russell, Kait O'Day, and Rory Ezell: Thank you for crafting with me, getting tattoos with me, and never making me feel like I'm too much.

I thank my official and unofficial mentors who have helped me grow from graduate school through the tenure track in a range of ways: Wendy Hesford, Beverly Moss, Treva Lindsey, Carmen Kynard, Mary Jo Reiff, Christina Cedillo, Amy Wan, Maryemma Graham, and Ersula Ore. The labor and thinking that informs my writing has been foundationally shaped by your scholarship, mentorship, and advice. I am grateful for all the truths you speak. To my rhet/comp friends who have become my real-life friends, I would not even bother to show my face at a conference if you weren't there. Specifically, I thank Anna Zeemont and Ruby Mendoza for always providing honest support and care.

My close friends and colleagues at the University of Kansas (KU), I could not have made it through without you. Abe Weil, thank you for helping me see when it's time to quit. I feel strong with you. Brian Atkinson, my first friend at KU: I'd never have survived without you. Misty Schieberle, same brain, I love texting you and saying the same things at the same time in the same place. Other colleagues and mentors at KU who have critically shaped my work as a scholar, academic, and professional: Darren Canady, Laura Mielke, Jon Lamb, Giselle Anatol, Marta Caminero, and Ayesha Hardison. Thank you. I am also deeply appreciative of the ways my mentees and graduate students at KU have forwarded and extended my thinking, not just in this book, but as a scholar writ large. I especially thank Brynn Fitzsimmons, Abby Breyer, Emily Counsil, Ayat Dashti, Sarah Thornsberry, Jade Harrison, and Kahill Perkins.

Without the material support of the KU Hall Center for Humanities Residential Fellowship, I could not have juggled my research, teaching, and advising responsibilities while working on this book. I am also very thankful to have had the support of the KU Department of English Shirley Cundiff and Jordan L. Haines Fellowship for two semesters to help further the completion of this project.

I thank the University Press of Colorado/Utah State University Press for providing a home for *The Benevolent Gaslight*. Without the mentorship and advocacy of former editor Rachael Levay, I can easily imagine a world in which this project and the vision behind it would not have come to fruition in the way it has today. Thank you, Rachael, not only for your unwavering commitment to academic and professional ethics, but also the time and labor you invested in developing and promoting this project. I also thank current editorial staff—in particular, Skylar Cooper and Michelle Chen—as well as the thoughtful anonymous peer reviewers who helped critically advance and sharpen the scholarly and political interventions of this project. Importantly, I'd also like to acknowledge the scholarly works that preceded and informed the thinking behind the content of this book. In particular, adapted excerpts from Lou and my coauthored article, " 'I Am Not Your Teaching Moment': The Benevolent Gaslight and Epistemic Violence" (2022), originally published in *College Composition and Communication*, and my single-authored article, "Backchannel Pedagogies: Unsettling Racial Teaching Moments and White Futurity" (2022), originally published in *Present Tense*, are featured in the preface, introduction, chapter 1, and chapter 3 of this book.

Finally, I thank my coauthor, Lou Maraj, for the years of collaborative knowledge-making that brought us here. I value the writing, research, and labor you have invested in this project.

The process of finishing this book was difficult, but it brought clarity. I have seen the creative ways powerful scholars utilize backchannel retaliation to intimidate and censor necessary critique. These retaliations, perhaps to the dismay of the actors who weaponize them, ironically continue to affirm the impact of projects like this. I have also come to realize, through the challenging dynamics that shaped this first book of my scholarly career, the im/possibilities of sustaining relationships depending on where one stands—in institutional power, in identity, in life—and of the multiple truths that inform collaborative work. For these critical realizations, I remain forever grateful.

With love,
Pritha

Index

About the Authors

Caribbean-born **Louis M. Maraj, PhD**, is a multi-award-winning scholar, multimedia artist, and author of *Black or Right: Anti/Racist Campus Rhetorics*. His critical/creative projects environ (anti)blackness and expressive form. Currently, he is an associate professor in University of British Columbia's School of Journalism, Writing & Media. Learn more at loumaraj.com.

Pritha Prasad, PhD, is an award-winning interdisciplinary scholar and teacher. Her work, which sits at the intersections of rhetoric and writing studies, critical ethnic studies, feminist and queer studies, and critical university studies, can be found in a range of publications, including *College Composition and Communication*, *Present Tense*, *Peitho*, and *Prose Studies*. In 2023, Prasad and Maraj were recipients of the Conference on College Composition and Communication (CCCC) Richard Braddock Award for their coauthored article, "'I Am Not Your Teaching Moment': The Benevolent Gaslight and Epistemic Violence" (2022), a project that centrally inspired the writing and research for this book. Prasad is currently an assistant professor and Conger-Gabel Teaching Professor in the Department of English at the University of Kansas.

www.ingramcontent.com/pod-product-compliance
Ingram Content Group UK Ltd.
Pitfield, Milton Keynes, MK11 3LW, UK
UKHW041841150726
7214IPUK00015B/103